CRUCIFYING THE CHRIST

Mark Gee

To Joanna, far more precious than gold!
(I'm glad it was you)

Also to Susanna & Luke, I love you both so much.

Forward

"There is no pit too deep, but God is deeper still." The truth in these words of Corrie ten Boom is graphically illustrated in Mark's moving and gripping story. He tells how God reached down to him when he was as low as he could get, and then did a wonderful work of salvation and renewal in the Holy Spirit.

But does it last?

Mark's conversion took place 25 years ago, and as his pastor and friend for the last 15 years I can assure you that Mark has kept to his promise that he would serve the God who had so wonderfully saved him all those years ago. He is now a happily married man, whose wife and children are his chief delight, after God. He is actively involved in Christian service, and is well respected within the church family.

Mark's desire in writing his story is that all the glory should go to God. I believe that he has succeeded in this aim, and I am delighted to commend this book to you.

Reverend Maurice Markham

PREFACE

Revelation 12:11
They overcame him by the blood of the Lamb
and by the word of their testimony;
they did not love their lives so much as to shrink from death.

It has taken me over twenty-five years to write this book. I have wanted
to write it many times, but was beaten back each time by a fear that if I
attempted it before I was ready, I would not be able to convey
accurately what happened without glamorising the events that occurred.
Age brings with it a certain amount of wisdom and humility, and if I
have discovered anything about these two elusive gifts - and it is a big
"if" - then the time is now to put pen to paper. My sole motivation was
to glorify the Lord, and I hope that I have done what I set out to
achieve, but only you can be the judge of that.

Please note: Most of the names contained herein associated with my
time in the Legión have been changed to protect the identity of those
with whom I served.

CHAPTER ONE

The Gods and Monsters of Legend

'Give me the child until he is seven, and I will give you the man'
A Jesuit proverb.

November 1983

I woke up cold and shivering. An insistent bitter wind throughout the night had frozen my bones, preventing the deep sleep my tired body craved. As I groaned and rubbed the sleep out of my eyes, the hostile reality of the new day dawned on me.

Desperation had forced me to try to find shelter and a decent night's sleep by some huts on the beach in Marbella, South-Eastern Spain. I sighed in despair. I had very little money, about four hundred pesetas to be exact, just over two pounds in English money, and I did not have a clue as to where I was going to find sufficient to get me through the rest of the day.

I did have some hashish though, enough for one last joint, so as I hunkered down in my donkey jacket and smoked the dope. I pondered my life up until this moment.

It wasn't a pretty picture.

*

I was born in Huddersfield, West Yorkshire. My mum was called Jacqueline, and she was only sixteen, much too young to be a wife never mind a mum. Not much older than her was my father, Neil Paradise. Early on in the marriage he decided that the best way to deal with his issues was to become violently drunk whenever he got the chance. I do not remember much about him, but from the few remaining photos I have of him I can see that he was good looking and well dressed. I guess that it takes more than style and a handsome face to be a good husband and father, a hard lesson my mum learnt very early on in the relationship.

Maybe my mum should have known better, after all, she was advised by everyone who knew her not to marry Neil, including, bizarrely, his own mother, who told her to stay away from him because he was "bad news"! However, we all know that since the world began, teenage hormones and a stubborn streak never did listen to reason. Needless to say, the relationship was not destined to last.

When I was three, and my mum a world-weary, battered nineteen year old, she took herself, me and my new baby brother, Glyn, back to her mum and dad's. Once back at her parents, my mum had no option but to go back to being a daughter, and Glyn and I automatically became surrogate sons to my nan and granddad.

Like most adults, I can remember very little about my early childhood before the age of three; just a few tangled memories, visible to me as if looking through thick fog. I also have to rely on the memories of what others around me observed, recollections that were talked about only when the mood of the gathering could take it. Things that were barely mentioned because the pain of them induced a memory that everyone concerned would rather were washed from the table of their memory. The sad fact is that, although I cannot recall most of these memories, it does not mean that they do not have power over me. Whatever it was I did see and hear during those early formative years must have been horrendous, because they continue to plague me to this day.

It is like that for all of us if we choose to accept fact. Infancy lies like a foundation stone in our memory, moulding and fashioning us into the adults we become later. Childhood should be a dream we remember as a time of laughter and innocence, a place where the gods are large and the monsters small. Unfortunately for some of us, the dream ends up becoming more like a nightmare, and before we know how to deal with the wickedness of those around us, we are already neck deep in corruption.

In my own personal world, my mum, nan and granddad were my gods, whereas my father, Neil, and the local kids who bullied me when I went to live with my grandparents, because I did not have a dad, were the monsters: monsters that seemed to have no other purpose in life but to destroy me. As did the headmistress of the local primary school I attended, who by taking a particularly bizarre and vicious dislike of me, and going out of her way to make my first school years as miserable as possible, only served to propagate my then tentative realisation that life was going to be a very painful and distressing experience.

In recent years I have spoken to a number of psychiatrists in search of closure and understanding, and they tell me that trauma can cause you to disappear inside your own mind, where the desire to protect yourself from further damage can cause you to create a make-believe world where you are safe from the demons of reality. As a child

I reacted no differently. I became a recluse; happy with what was in my own head, and more often than not horribly disturbed by what was outside it. I became a dreamer - I still am. It is hard to shake off such early indoctrination. This, the early part of my life story, as crazy and out of the ordinary as it is, is the product of my desire to find an adventure that would help me make sense of the world around me.

My nan and granddad were a godsend, but by the time they started to have an influence in my life I was already an extremely screwed up child. By their actions they persuaded me to take a look at the real world every now and then. They let me believe that life might have something better to offer me than what I had previously been served up. From them there was no rejection, no violence, no blame offered, which I could use to castigate myself. Just love, unreserved and unconditional. I have never experienced anything else from them from the first time I met them until now.

Yet in spite of this love being heaped upon me so unconditionally, it was becoming obvious to everyone that I was heading for trouble. Even before starting school I was being brought home by the police for one piece of high jinks or another. One of the policemen when handing me over to my increasingly frazzled mother ominously declared, "You have a big problem there!" He was obviously someone who knew what he was talking about. However, I remember little about being so naughty, what I remember most about that time with my grandparents is being loved. It was tangible, and compared to the emotional carnage I was used to it was like paradise.

My granddad owned his own business making sausage skins. A true Yorkshireman who called a spade a spade and lived by the maxim that "where there's muck there's brass". He was overweight most of his life, and up until he had a heart attack that shocked him out of it, he smoked over sixty cigarettes a day. He loved his food and he also liked a drink. He worked hard and he worshipped my nan. Providing for her and making her comfortable seemed to be his only real joy in life. I have nothing but fond memories of him, and I still miss him, he was a true god of my childhood memory.

My nan is still alive, aged as I pen this a fabulous ninety-nine years old. She still lives in her own home, and although her body is letting her down a little, her mind is still as sharp as a pin. I will always remember her as a dignified and strikingly good-looking woman, who would not even step out of the house to put the washing on the line without putting on her lipstick. She has told me many stories about her early life as the daughter of a village blacksmith and, like my granddad, she was brought up in a working class family where the day-to-day struggles to feed and clothe the family were an ever present reality.

They were wonderfully normal, with no airs or pretension to distil their honest no-frills humanity, and they seemed to love me for whom I was. They brought a sense of normality to my life, and I still look back to my time in their care as my childhood golden years; a time where the freedom of childhood was not too badly damaged or impinged by the callous and indifferent actions of those around me.

My mum has always found it hard to share about what she went through with Neil, so my grandparents were the ones who answered my questions. They told me what happened before they took my mum and her two sons back into their home. They told me about the beatings and the tears, the suicide attempts and the terror their daughter underwent at the hands of a man she tried so hard to love. They also told me how I had to wear a crucifix splint because it was discovered that I had a dislocated hip when I was a few months old, and they laughed out loud at the memories they had of me attempting anything and everything I could, even though I was so physically encumbered. They also told me how horribly disturbed a three-year-old child I was then when I came to live with them, and how wretched and unable to help they felt in the face of such damage.

I would have stayed with them forever if given the chance, but life does not always give you what you want, and after a few years my mum, who was anxious to become her own woman again, found a man she liked. He was called Colin Gee, eleven years her senior. One night she informed me and Glyn that he was going to be our new dad. I remember my first meeting with him well. He was tall, well dressed in a three-piece wool suit, and he looked very stern and nervous as he struggled to smile at me. My mum was keen for us to get on, and all might have been well in other circumstances. There was great potential for good to come from the coming together, but sometimes relationships clash, and so unfortunately did mine with Colin.

He was a divorcee, with children from his first marriage that he had to forgo when he left his first wife. It would not be untrue to say that he had a lot of emotional issues caused by the acrimonious divorce he had been through, and one of the things that must have hurt was the fact that in place of his own two children he got me and Glyn. It could not have been easy for him to inherit two, mixed up crazy kids merely because he had fallen in love with my mum, and he truly loved her, of that there has never been any doubt.

Here though I must admit that I was a very difficult child to handle, and it must have been hard for Colin coping with the kid I was then when there was no genetic bond to help us both through such difficulties. He tried, as did I at times, but we really clashed very badly, and I got it into my head that he hated me. I suppose it did not help that Colin was from a generation that found it hard to display their emotions easily.

Now, sitting here writing this book, I know that he did not hate me, he was purely unable to cope. I was headstrong and aggressive, and as I grew older, angry at everyone and everything. I do not think it an understatement to say that I would have tried the patience of a saint. The worst part of the whole scenario was that after taking the rejection of my real father very personally, I now had Colin's repudiation to cope with, another stick to beat myself with, and I fell into the trap of blaming myself for everything that went wrong thereafter.

I must not paint too dramatic a picture here, or deliberately paint things too dark. That would be unjust. There were some good times, happy respites when the clouds cleared and a picture of a normal happy family was tentatively painted on our emotionally bloodstained canvas. I particularly remember that we had some good holidays, and I confess that I never lacked material things such as toys and clothes. Outwardly I was a privileged child.

Once, amazingly, Colin even saved my life.

*

I was thirteen, and sledging on the local golf course one glorious winter's day when the snow lay twelve inches deep on the ground. It was like a bridal gown thrown over the green fields, cloaking everything with the white virgin innocence of its mantle. All throughout that long and happy day - that saw me go home only to eat and to scratch the chilblains in my feet until they nearly bled - I helped some older lads develop a sledge run through some trees on a wickedly steep part of the course we had commandeered as our playground.

Night was falling, and with it the temperature. This had the effect of turning our route into almost sheet ice. I could see that it was becoming dangerous, and I didn't want to make a final run before it became too dark to see, but egged on by the others I mounted my sledge and set off downhill.

I quickly realised I was in trouble when I discovered I could not steer. I lost control and hit a tree at something in the region of fifty miles an hour. The large wooden sledge was a write-off, and so was I nearly. I did not know it then, but I had ruptured my spleen and was bleeding internally. I staggered back home thinking that I had merely been winded, not knowing that I had mere hours to live.

In the night I awoke to go to the toilet a few times, only to pass out on each occasion. Every time I tried to stand up the lights would go out and I would find myself back on the floor. My parents quickly called an ambulance after noticing that my pupils were severely dilated.

At the hospital, after four or five hours of being prodded and probed, the doctor assigned to me decided that there was nothing wrong, and asked Colin if he thought I was "putting it on". Thankfully Colin, who was valiantly trying to keep me awake, could see that by then I was in serious pain, and demanded a second opinion. Once seen by the second doctor, Colin was informed that I had minutes to live. They barged me into emergency theatre and operated. I had lost four pints of blood, and was a whisker away from death.

So I owe him my life, and for that I am grateful, and it was times like that that convinced me what happened between myself and Colin was nothing more than a clash of personalities. You cannot save the life of someone you truly loathe. We just did not like each other, and that stupidity we were never able to overcome. Unfortunately, none of the material things I had, or the brief moments when we got along, or even the fact that he saved my life, could undo the fact that I did not feel loved, and it was this one thing that undid me so utterly and completely.

I was constantly getting into trouble at school for fighting or being disrespectful. I was touchy, emotionally insecure and prone to severe bouts of mind-numbing anger and depression. I was becoming a basket case, a time bomb just waiting to explode. Neither did it help that I started to manifest violent similarities to my real father, Neil, and this frightened my mum, who made the rather unwise decision to tell me constantly that I was "just like my real dad".

This had a very negative effect on me as you can imagine. I hated my real father. I hated what he had done to my mum, and I hated what he had done to me and Glyn. To be told that I was just like him caused me to detest myself with an even deeper passion. I could not bear the thought that I would turn out like him, but it seemed almost inevitable. My transformation into what I hated was like a demonic prophecy being fulfilled in front of my own eyes.

Needless to say, we had become a very dysfunctional family, and by the time I entered my teens I was already the black sheep of the family, virtually an outcast. This angered me more than I can mention. You hear a lot about troubled children "crying out for attention", and I do not think that I was any different. I could not make any sense of anything. Life did not seem to hold anything worth having. I desperately wanted to be happy, to be "normal", but all I seemed to get was misery and pain.

By this time books had become my one true love. I was capable of devouring a book a day, especially during the school holidays when the local library became a world of such glorious potential that I felt like Aladdin entering the genie's cave every time I climbed the stone steps and pushed open the thick oak doors to enter. Adventure books were my favourites, and I often longed with an ache that made my stomach hurt, to have such an adventure for myself. It was the only thing I could think of happening to me that would make any sense of anything.

Rock music also started to feature heavily in my life, and although it never came close to usurping books for my affections, I grew to love it. Locked in my bedroom with the headphones on and the volume turned up so loud I could hardly bear it, I closed my eyes and surrendered myself to the music. I found the aggressive guitars and the angst that underpinned its lyrics something that resonated easily with my troubled soul. Groups such as AC/DC, Black Sabbath, Deep Purple, Status Quo and Led Zepplin became my idols. Their lyrics fuelled my resentment, and I could lose myself in their music for hours on end.

My only other respite seemed to come from the countryside around me. After they married, my mum and Colin moved to a beautiful village called Meltham, not far from Holmfirth, a place made famous by the sitcom Last of the Summer Wine. My playground became the woods, moors and reservoirs that surrounded me, and I was never happier than when I was alone exploring them, or out on my bike careering at breakneck speed down the perilously steep hills. It was here that my love of the English countryside, especially its wildlife, grew and blossomed. No matter what my problems were, as soon as I was out of the house and lost in the green paradise that was my own personal piece of Yorkshire, I immediately felt lighter.

Unfortunately I always had to go back home; and things were not getting any easier. By this time I was off the rails and heading for God alone knows where. I had no self-control and no respect for myself or anyone else. My mum was on antidepressants, living in fear of the phone during the day, because more often than not it was the school phoning to tell her that I was in trouble again. Only her constantly begging me to "keep the peace" with Colin, and the fact that they found a boarding school for me when I was thirteen, prevented what could have been murder.

My one saving grace was that I had a half-decent brain; this gift enabled me to pass the entrance exam to the boarding school in question. It was called Trinity House Navigation School and was sited next to Princes Dock in Kingston-upon-Hull. The school took boys from the age of thirteen who wanted to join the Merchant Navy when they left school. It trained them in subjects such as seamanship and navigation as well as the usual core subjects like maths and English. Trinity House Cadets were highly prized by shipping companies who wanted apprentice officers with a head start in what it was going to be like at sea.

Up until I realised that this school was an opportunity to leave my family behind I had never considered the possibility of a life at sea, but I soon warmed to the idea. Surprisingly, this school has some fond memories for me, mainly because it was a strict place where they set well-defined boundaries that, for the most part, I was happy to live within. Plus I was away from home for most of the time, and that was most welcome. However, if you asked those who taught me about my sojourn in their midst, I do not think their memories will be as affectionate.

I was trouble. I was also confused and angry - very angry. Life was a bitch to which I was being forced into a marriage I did not want.

Some intellectuals say that you get what you wish for: that there is a power in the universe available to all men, and this power moulds life into whatever it is you want it to be. I knew that I wanted something out of the ordinary; I wanted an adventure right out of Hollywood. That was how I made sense of the anger and pain that writhed within me like a snake in my belly. The belief that somewhere out there, somewhere beyond the horizon of the monotony and boredom that plagued me, there was a voyage waiting for me. Something I could believe in and belong to. It became an obsession. I knew it was out there. I could almost taste it. All I had to do was find it.

As far as the rest of the world was concerned though, I was a screw-up, and if my parents had succumbed to the many head teachers' requests at all the schools I attended for me to see a child psychiatrist, whoever it was examining me would have had a field day, but they refused, and I'm glad they did. I think a psychiatrist would have twisted me up more than I already was. I knew I was different though, just not sure how or why. Mostly I knew that I was sadder and madder than most of my contemporaries.

A lot of my anger came from envy, and what hurt most, and what didn't seem fair to me at all, was that life for others seemed to be so much easier. As I watched and listened to my peers, it was as if they were living in another universe. Their lives were places that held laughter and happiness, and I could not understand why for me, just existing was becoming such an intolerable burden.

My sadness plummeted to new depths when the hormones of my teenage years started to take effect. One night, when I was fourteen, as the wind howled outside and the giant oak trees opposite my bedroom window swung and groaned in the face of a huge storm, I held a razor blade to my left wrist.

For hours I sat there, well into the night, mesmerised by the thought of what could come from my actions. I tried to summon up the determination to slice down, imagining the sleep of death, the peace that would come when my eyes closed one final time on the world.

Maybe death was the adventure I craved?

'Just slice down once with anger,' I whispered as the sweat dripped from my brow onto the end of my nose and then down onto the carpet, forming a damp patch at my feet. 'Just once,' I pleaded as my muscles tensed, preparing themselves to push down into the soft yielding flesh and bring forth my release.

Just one fraction of a second's worth of determination and I could die.

I couldn't do it, and the shame of my cowardice only heightened my anger and depression. This was more than a cry for attention, because if it had been merely a cry I would have done something to tell people how sad I was. Yet I told no one about how close I came to death, or how tired I was of life. It became my own guilty secret.

It is a strange thing to wake up the morning after seriously contemplating killing yourself. The circumstances that drove you to such a desperate consideration are still there. No one has changed, and there is still no one to tell, no shoulder to cry on. The world around you treats you exactly the same as it did the day before, and you feel hopelessly trapped in the inadequacy of life. It is as if nothing matters any more. Life is only death waiting to happen.

Life did go on, however, in spite of my hidden desire to exit it, and even after being expelled from school for fighting, I somehow managed to get enough O levels to find a job as a navigating officer apprentice in the British Merchant Navy. Both the school and I breathed a sigh of relief as I walked out of its doors and into a life on the ocean wave. Everyone I left behind had me down in their year book as the one most likely to be dead before he was twenty-one, either by his own hand or someone else's. If offered decent odds I might have had a flutter on that eventuality myself.

By this time I didn't really care what happened to me. As long as I got the adventure I was longing for, I was unconcerned. In books the best adventures always involved death anyway, and if I didn't have the guts to do the job myself, maybe if I put myself in enough dangerous circumstances they would do the job for me.

CHAPTER TWO

A Fickle Mistress

Eternal Father, strong to save, whose arm has bound the restless wave.
Who bidd'st the mighty ocean deep, its own appointed limits keep.
Oh hear us when we cry to thee,
For those in peril on the sea.

Rev William Whiting 1860

I joined my first ship in Pakistan. She was called the Ripon Grange and was a bulk carrier at anchor due to discharge its load of grain in Karachi. What followed was one hell of a first trip for any boy. From Karachi we sailed to South Africa, where we loaded up with coal we part discharged in both Genoa and Venice. From there we sailed out of the Mediterranean and bunkered up in the Canary Islands, then crossed the Atlantic to load up with grain in Argentina. Sailing east we bunkered up again in Cape Town where I was paid off and flown home. The ship was going on to Japan via Singapore, and I was desperate to stay on it.

I loved it. I didn't want to leave. I begged to be allowed to stay, but I had been on-board for seven months and technically that was longer than was allowed, so I had to leave.

Once home, I phoned up after two weeks of the seven weeks leave due to me and asked for another ship as soon as they could get me one.

I loved the sea and life on-board. I loved the changeable faces of the oceans according to their fickle and sometimes violent moods. There are so many colours of blue and green on the ocean that you run out of words, and she is so unpredictable as to turn from flat calm to tempestuous in a matter of minutes. The sea is truly marvellous to behold, and I loved it with a passion. Even now I still dream about being at sea, there is a freedom there I grew to love, and still miss.

Although frightened, I remember laughing out loud once as the cargo ship I was on was pitched to and fro like a cork in a bucket as we bore out the tail end of a hurricane in the Caribbean. The ship that had seemed too huge as we had sailed through the flat calm waters of the Sargasso Sea towards Bermuda a few days before was now being thrown about like a kid's toy boat in the bath. The waves were colossal, smashing down onto us like giant watery fists as we hove-to. As other men prayed, I laughed. Danger, any danger, seemed to wake me up. I knew that I should have been as terrified as everyone else, but I was seemingly incapable of fear without enjoying it. I never seemed to be more alive than when I came face to face with my own mortality.

One other thing I loved was the camaraderie amongst the crew. On-board a ship you are thrown together with others, and although we were all individuals with diverse interests and personalities, we all shared a common interest - the sea and the welfare of the ship we sailed on. At sea I felt as if I was a part of something bigger than myself. I felt as if I belonged. It was a good feeling.

Most of all though, I loved the fact that I was always moving, never staying still, liking the changing horizons, and always wondering what was over the next one, whether it would be what I was looking for. It never was, but sometimes things I saw came close to assuaging the tumult in my soul.

One particular occasion I saw a sunset that hangs in my memory like the words of a favourite song, or the memory of my first kiss. We were sailing along the coast of Yemen heading for the Arabian Gulf. The sun was sinking down below the horizon, but it was no ordinary sunset. The sun was casting thousands of vivid reds, yellows and oranges into the sky, lighting up the twilight like a log fire. The sea was a beautiful, light azure blue, with the wave tops a creamy iridescent green, the subtle colours of which reminded me of the wings of a kingfisher I had once seen back in Yorkshire as she had flitted in and out of view faster than a bullet.

The wind was light and fresh, sufficient only to balance out the heat of the declining day. Dolphins played around the bow wave like the crazy sea-borne children they are, full of a joy I truly envied. Flying fish also broke through the waves like sea-to-air missiles, skimming away on the surface for hundreds of feet, away from the underwater danger our approach had triggered.

It was a blissfully dramatic scene, and even the most seasoned sailors out on deck watching the magnificent display that sundown was throwing up for us were struck dumb by the beauty of it.

Transfixed, I made my way up to the fo'c's'le and sat down by the anchor cables with a beer and a cigarette. I drank in the sight until the sun set and the sky fell dark. It was like something out of a real life fantasia, and for a while, as I sipped the beer and smoked, everything was cool and all right with the world.

This was not always the case though, because unfortunately for me the social life of the ship was in the bar, and if you give a young, mixed-up sixteen-year-old boy like me the opportunity to drink without restraint he will take it. I quickly found solace and comfort in alcohol. At first it was a novelty, something that did not seem to affect me all that much. Gradually though, it began to overpower me (maybe "infect" is a more suitable word that best describes what became of me). I became a slave to drink and could not even contemplate going to bed sober. Drink became a crutch, and I found that after a while I could not walk without it.

A few spells at Hull Nautical College where I studied for my second mate's certificate, and where I shamefully drank and womanised my way through my studies, without much care or concern for the mates I drank with or the girls I slept with, only served to ratchet up the tension in my soul. Tighter and tighter the depression became until it was almost unbearable. I yearned for freedom, but everything I did fastened the chains binding me tighter still.

The strange thing is that all should have been well. I was on the launch pad of a life and career others my age would have given their right arm for, so why, with the world seemingly at my feet, did I get so wasted one night at college on cocaine, beer and whisky, and take the now familiar razor blade to the back of my left arm and slash it repeatedly? I can barely remember doing it, and only started to understand fully what had happened to me as I was receiving over fifty stitches from a pretty nurse in the hospital.

A few more trips on various vessels from gas tankers to cargo ships saw me hit my twentieth birthday, and along with the world's oceans I also saw my fair share of skid rows and whores' bedrooms. I was smoking dope frequently. I was also popping acid, smoking heroin and snorting cocaine whenever the opportunity arose: most of the time though, I drank. Anytime, anyplace anywhere, I would never say no to a beer. This left me with the DTs on the very few occasions I went more than three days without a drink, along with an aching desire to rip out my insides and start my life all over again.

Drink is a strange companion. I felt unclean when sober and worse drunk, yet all I wanted was to get blasted at every opportunity that raised itself. Nothing I could say on this page would adequately describe what it is to be an alcoholic, and I have seriously mulled over what to tell you about this time in my life, because if I fully opened the pages of my memory I could turn these few short paragraphs into their own book. However, I have decided that such excess would perhaps glamorise what was, in effect, me sinking into a pit of despair.

Suffice to say that the more I looked for life at the bottom of a bottle the more I lost myself. I had no idea where I was going or what I wanted from life, but I gradually realised that if I stayed at sea I would die, both physically and emotionally. It was becoming obvious that the adventure I was looking for was not going to be found on any one of the seven seas.

Fortunately, circumstances conspired to overtake me before I could leave voluntarily. The British Merchant Navy, like most British industry at that time, was floundering because of cheap foreign competition, and I was made redundant. This left me without a plan or any real desire for life. I had nowhere to go. I was lost, and for the first time in my life, I knew I was.

Going home to Meltham was not an option; I was still at loggerheads with Colin, as one particular fracas demonstrated, almost completely destroying the tentative relationship to which we were still clinging.

On leave for my eighteenth birthday I spent a weekend in the cells at the local police station. It was after a particularly vicious argument with Colin, and all the anger I had within me exploded like a landmine. I smashed up the house and came very close to putting Colin in hospital. I finished the night by venting my anger on a few local shop windows with a large plank of wood, before the local constabulary arrived to take me away.

No, I could not go home, nor did I want to. Home was not home. I knew that now. It never had been. I had to find another place to belong.

*

For a short time I shared a rented house with Glyn in a rundown mill village called Slaithewaite. There I knocked about with some bikers, drank a lot, did some drugs and worked in a cardboard box factory until they sacked me. Eventually my relationship with Glyn soured, mainly because of my inability to treat anyone close to me decently. I had also started to find the expectations and reality of the sort of life I was living tedious in the extreme anyway. There was no adventure there, just monotony and tedium as one day followed another in its dreadful inevitability. I borrowed some money from a bank I had no intention of paying back, bought a motorbike and set off on my travels, resolving, scarily and way too casually, that if I could find nothing worth living for I would kill myself.

I smashed up the bike in an accident on the Isle of Wight after missing a stop sign while tripping on magic mushrooms. In the midst of the wreckage, which I was lucky to survive with nothing worse than a twisted knee, I quickly realised that because I had no licence, no insurance and no MOT, I would get the book thrown at me when the police came knocking, so I left the wrecked bike by the side of the road and ran off to London. Maybe there, in the midst of its fabled opportunity, I could find what it was I was looking for.

*

London, the City of Dreams - I felt like it was going to be my last hope.

After sleeping rough for a few days, and nursing a depression so dark it was engulfing me, I realised that London did not have whatever it was I was looking for. With my last few pound notes I bought myself a bottle of whisky and two cartons of paracetamol. My demise I decided, would take place in Leicester Square, surrounded by indifferent people and the bright lights of a world that I wanted to spit in the face of. As I unscrewed the cap of the bottle and prepared to swill down a handful of pills with the first mouthful, a Hare Krishna tapped me on the shoulder. Deciding that this had to be fate, I accepted his invitation back to their temple in Soho.

I was adrift, on the verge of death, and suddenly these people, with their smiles and their concern, offered me a new start. Naturally I took it. I was in no state to argue with someone who told me that they had all the answers. After a short stay at Bhaktivedanta Manor, the London headquarters George Harrison of "The Beatles" fame had bought them on the outskirts of London, I enrolled as a "devotee of Krishna". I was then taken to a place called Chaitanya College; a magnificent stately home near Worcester, bought by the Krishnas to be used as a training facility for their UK operation.

This was not my first introduction to religion. With the birth of Jason, my parent's first and only child together, they made an attempt to continue going to church after having him baptised. It was a local parish church in a village called Wilshaw not far from Meltham. I found it to be a cold and austere place, and never felt comfortable there.

I cannot say that I had never felt close to God, or doubted His existence. As far back as I can remember I have had a faith. Maybe that was because my mother had prayed the Lord's Prayer with me every night, or because every school I went to had assembly and Bible teaching. I do not know whether this is something someone is born with or is taught, I will have to leave that to the theologians. What I do know is that I found it impossible to ascribe the world, its contents and my own existence down to a mere act of random chance as was touted by the atheists and evolutionists, but neither could I connect with the "God" the Church of England wanted me to accept. He was too distant, too clouded in indifference and alien to the world I inhabited. I decided that if there was a God, He was nothing like this one; and if He was, I did not want to know Him.

This was not to say that the "idea" of Christianity had not succeeded in touching me emotionally every now and then. There were times when the idea of God seemed very real. Such as when there was a film about the Passion on television and I would find myself teary-eyed as Christ was led away to be crucified, or when I was in the chapel at Trinity House School singing the school hymn "For Those in Peril on the Sea", finding my heart strangely moved within me for no reason I fully understood. Also once when so completely wasted on a mixture of pills and alcohol I found myself in the Hull Seaman's Mission Chapel being ministered to by the Catholic priest there. It was a strangely bizarre and humbling time, as the kind priest I had so rudely awakened from his bed at two o'clock in the morning prayed for me with a genuine sincerity, totally unconcerned about the fact that I was barely conscious from drink.

These moments were a long way from deliberately seeking out an answer to the question of life, or methodically devoting myself to the pursuit of God. There was a tremendous gulf between the God I wanted to believe in and the one that was on offer. Sadly neither did anyone I know demonstrate any true sincerity about religion; consequently, I never took it seriously.

Here though the Hare Krishnas demonstrated something different. They were passionate about what they believed, and they were prepared to back up what they believed by the way they lived. Amongst them my eyes were opened to the fact that there was a spiritual dimension to life I had not truly considered in any depth. Consequently, I threw myself into the life and tried hard to be a good "devotee", to follow their rules; and to convince myself as I chanted "Hare Krishna" that I was on the road to enlightenment, but every time I bowed down to the idols in the temple, I felt my conscience prick me, and a voice within would often cry out:

'You should try Jesus first.'

Maybe the voice came from the fact that although I had rejected the Christianity of the Church of England, I still considered myself to be a Christian. Maybe the voice was from somewhere more sublime and gracious. I would rather believe the latter. Now my eyes had opened to the possibility that there was a God who might have some answers for me, so my "searching" took on a whole new impetus. I left the Hare Krishnas and resolved to work my way across Europe to Israel, where I would seek out Jesus Christ. I had heard about Kibbutz living, and was interested in trying to find out exactly what that was all about, besides, if I could not find God in the Holy Land, where else would I find Him?

It wasn't really a plan though, it was more like a daydream, and maybe because of the drugs, or maybe because of the state my mind was in, I thought that by merely "drifting" I would end up where I was supposed to be. I caught the first bus I saw, wherever it was going, and irrespective of its destination I boarded the first train leaving at whatever train station I was at.

When hitchhiking, wherever the driver was going, who stopped to give me a lift, also became my next stop. I was going nowhere and somewhere, and all the while I was going to wherever it was the wind was blowing me I hoped it would be the place that held whatever it was I was looking for.

*

The wind had brought me here, to southern Spain; to a frozen beach and a place where I had no money and no future, to a place where I was once again left wondering why I had got myself into a situation that was the result of me just not caring whether I lived or died. Here I was again at the crossroads, and this time I knew with a terrifying certainty that either I found something worth living for, or I would die.

I was running out of options.

So much for my life up until now, I thought, as I shivered in the face of the cold wind tearing in from the Mediterranean. I should have been in Israel seeking God, instead here I was in Spain wondering what the hell today was going to bring that could possibly make my life any worse. I had drifted instead of focusing on where I should have been going, and I was down and out again, but this time I was down and out in a foreign country - much worse.

I sighed and flicked the end of the roach into the sand and decided on a wander around Marbella to see what was happening. Maybe something would turn up.

By this time it was ten in the morning, and the only place I found within my price range was a small cafe where I bought a cheese sandwich and a small coffee. The barman gave me one hundred and eighty-eight pesetas change, roughly a pound. It was to prove to be a very significant amount of money indeed.

I took my time eating and drinking as I eyed up the few guys in the bar, wondering whether any one of them might know where I could get some work. Most of them were expats. Eventually I approached a couple to ask if they knew where I might earn a few quid. I was asked what I had done before and when I said Merchant Navy, one of them pulled me to one side and sat me down in a quiet corner of the bar.

He was furtive and was obviously checking out my story. He asked loads of questions and I started to wonder whether he was wasting my time before he eventually came out with it. He said that he could get me work making two or three trips to Morocco every month. The boats used were high speed powerboats, the cargo cannabis resin, and the pay was two thousand US dollars a trip.

I was tempted, and as he went back to the bar to get me a drink, another one of the men I had spoken to came over to me.

'You could join the Legión,' he said.

Thinking that he meant the French Foreign Legion, I replied that I didn't have enough money to make the fare to France.

He merely laughed.

'No, mate,' he said, 'you could join the Spanish Legión. They take foreigners, and they have a base up in the mountains not far from here near Ronda. Be warned though, they are one of the toughest regiments in the world. The training and lifestyle are brutal, only the hardest survive.'

I was intrigued, and totally unconcerned about the brutal aspect of the life. My life was not exactly a bed of roses at the moment anyway. Most importantly, the Foreign Legión sounded like adventure, and it was certainly a better option than spending the rest of my life rotting in a Spanish or Moroccan prison if caught drug running.

'How can I get there?' I asked.

'The bus station is just up the road,' he replied.

'Thanks,' I said as I stood up and made my way out of the bar without a second glance.

The one way ticket to Ronda cost me one hundred and eight-seven pesetas. I was left with the clothes I stood up in and one peseta in my pocket.

Still, it wasn't all bad. I was going to join the Foreign Legión! Maybe they could make something of me.

*

A few months later I heard that over twenty tonnes of hashish had been found by the police in caves to the south of Marbella. The gang, headed up by British expats, were sentenced to lengthy jail terms. Apparently they had been bringing the drug in from Morocco on high speed powerboats.

CHAPTER THREE

A Bus Ride to Fate

Legionarios a Luchar, Legionarios a Morir.
Legionarios to the Fight, Legionarios to the Death.

I tried to make the bus driver understand that I wanted to go to the Legión barracks near Ronda, but my Spanish language skills were non-existent. Only after he handed me a pen and some paper and I wrote "Legión" on it did he smile and nod his head. I don't know how long the journey took; I must have fallen asleep, because the next thing I remember was someone shaking me by the shoulder. Everyone on the bus, including the driver, was looking at me. Word must have got around about my destination.

Bleary eyed I looked out of the window; there at the top of a hill was an entrance to a barracks. A soldier stood guard, and on the arch above his head was written "Legionarios a Luchar, Legionarios a Morir".

I thanked the driver and got off the bus, watching as it pulled away in a great cloud of diesel fumes. There was nowhere else to go now; the one peseta I had in my pocket was not going to get me anywhere, so I nervously made my way up the hill, hoping the guys at the top were on a recruiting drive.

The guard looked smart and very fierce in his olive green combat uniform with black leather cartridge pouches, belt and shiny brass buckle. A semi-automatic assault rifle was slung casually across his chest, and the famous Legión cap, the "Chapiri", was perched boldly on his head, its distinctive red tassel hanging languidly above his right eye.

'I would like to join up,' I said, in English.

He obviously didn't speak English, and I definitely didn't speak Spanish, so I touched first his jacket then my own and told him again that I wanted to become a legionario.

He smiled broadly and shouted out behind him.

It didn't take long for a small and angry-looking sergeant to come out. He looked me up and down, and asked me a few questions I did not understand. After some more sign language I convinced him that I was a serious recruit. He brightened up considerably at the news and took me into the empty guard-post. He even gave me a cigarette and indicated that I should sit down. When he had gone I smoked the fag, coughing as the harsh black tobacco legionarios were famous for smoking hit my lungs, and took stock of my surroundings.

It was an austere room consisting of five three-tier bunks and a wooden table with half a dozen chairs. There was no fire, and no colour apart from the hand painted Legión mottos on the wall. It was cold and stern, and for the first time I wondered what it was I was doing here. I told myself that it was not too late to walk out of the front door; I had not signed anything yet. Yet even as the thought came to me I discounted it. For the first time in my life I knew that I was on the verge of a very big adventure, and I didn't want to miss it by wimping out.

An hour or two passed. Eventually the sergeant returned with someone who was obviously an officer. The sergeant indicated that I should stand up. I did so as the officer looked me up and down imperiously. In hesitant English, he then asked me what nationality I was and why I wanted to join. I told him that I was English and I wanted to join because I was looking for some adventure. He smiled and nodded to the sergeant, who looked pleased by my response, and left.

A few minutes later a jeep came to take me away. The sergeant shook my hand and gave me another cigarette as I climbed into the back. Along with the driver there was also a guard, complete with assault rifle and a tired smile. I had no idea where I was going or what was going to be expected of me, but if they had decided I needed an armed guard to get me there I didn't want to argue.

The guard was non-communicative, preferring to smoke and behave as if he had seen it all before. The driver, however, was more than happy to fill me in on my fate, and he did so in a loud "Spanglish" I guessed he had learnt in the tourist industry. After a while I came to understand that basic training was not going to be a picnic. He kept reinforcing the point by raising his right hand and making a chopping sound as he sucked in air over his teeth. You didn't need to be an expert at sign language to know what that meant.

The journey took about twenty minutes, and we finally pulled up at the entrance to another camp. This one also had the familiar arch, on which was written what I had now deduced was the Legión motto. "Legionarios a Luchar, Legionarios a Morir". I would have to find somebody to tell me what that meant before too long. I was also rather hoping that they would take a more tolerant approach to discipline when it came to a foreigner who had yet to learn the language.

After a short while I was shepherded into an administrative building and asked by yet another officer who spoke passable English why I wanted to join. I told him exactly what I had told the first. It was good enough. They took my passport from me, which I never saw again, and told me that I was to have a medical, whereupon subject to my health being okay I would sign a contract as a soldier of fortune owing my allegiance to the Spanish flag, after which I would be posted to a basic training company.

It took a couple of days before the medical was organised, and during this time I was bunked in an empty barracks with a half dozen other recruits. Mercifully one of them was an Algerian who spoke very good English. He helped me get to grips with the language. He also told me about certain aspects of Legión etiquette, and about what was, and what was not expected of me. On the whole it sounded like "do everything you are told to do quickly and without hesitation, or you will incur the violent wrath of the sergeants".

In most armies of the world, it is the NCOs who run things and keep everything operational. The Legion was no different, except that in the Spanish Legión, unlike the British Army or any other of the western world's armed forces, the sergeants and corporals were allowed to administer beatings at their own discretion. Sergeants in most armies of the world were not allowed to carry their own personal handguns, unlike in the Legión. If they did not want the standard army issue Star 9mm semi-automatic, they could purchase their own. Some even sported Magnum 44s.

It soon became obvious to me that the NCOs did not merely administer the law, they were the law, and it was not long before I saw my first example of a Legión NCO's disciplinary procedure.

I was waiting in the food queue for lunch when a legionario ran past a sergeant without saluting correctly. The sergeant called him back. The unfortunate legionario stood to attention as he was publicly berated by the fuming sergeant. Suddenly, and without warning, the sergeant punched him savagely in the solar plexus. The poor lad hit the deck with a cry of pain. I was shocked and looked around me to see what others made of it. No one batted an eyelid. The sergeant continued shouting until the unfortunate soldier got back up onto his feet. Grimacing painfully he then executed a perfect salute. The sergeant seemed satisfied and shooed him on his way.

I made a mental note to correctly salute everyone with stripes or pips as soon as I had been shown how.

Later that day we were taken for our first shower. I was looking forward to a good wash, having gone a week or two without one. What happened next was not what I expected at all. The shower assemblage itself consisted of a huge cold water tank on a wooden tower feeding twelve shower heads inside a tent, with a duckboard covering a mud floor. We were ordered to strip, thrown a block of soap, a threadbare towel, and told we had exactly one minute under the nozzle.

The temperature up in the Andalucian Mountains at that particular time of year was near zero, well below at night, and the water only fractionally warmer, any colder and it would probably have frozen. The soap was a gritty carbolic type that with which it was impossible to get a good lather, and the towels so old and thin they soaked up nothing. To make matters worse, we then had to wait until everyone else had finished showering before being allowed to dress. I was so cold my teeth were chattering and my lips were blue.

The strange thing is that afterwards, when I had warmed up, I felt completely invigorated. To this day, whenever I shower, I always flick the switch to cold for the last couple of minutes. It wakes up your body and mind like nothing else on earth.

There was one other unexpected silver lining to this particular dark cloud. Thanks to being ordered to strip I became an instant celebrity because of my many tattoos. I had accumulated the collection of eagles and Union Jacks during my time in the navy and my spell as a biker in Yorkshire. Most legionarios had tattoos, but they were of poor quality, often home-made in black ink with nothing more sophisticated than a hand-held needle and Indian ink. My multicoloured and professionally done ones were universally admired. It won me friends and a constant supply of cigarettes as lads came from all over the camp to admire the artwork.

I was pleased at my new found celebrity status, and it helped to pass the time as I waited for the medical. During this lull I also tried to pick up as much as I could by observation.

It became obvious that the Legión did everything at the double. They never walked when they could run, and the speed they marched at amazed me. I had been told previously that the Durham Light Infantry marched at the fastest pace in the world, keeping up one hundred and forty paces a minute. This is incorrect; the Spanish Legión is the fastest, marching at between one hundred and sixty and one hundred and eighty paces a minute depending on what sort of mood they were in, and the drill they are capable of at this speed is astonishing.

The more I saw of them the more I longed for a uniform, to become one of them. They were obviously some of the hardest men I had ever laid my eyes on, and I knew that I could find my position amongst them given half a chance.

The more I also learnt about Legión culture, the more I decided I liked that too. One of the Legión hymns is called "El Novio de la Muerte", "The Bridegroom of Death", and a pictorial depiction of the hymn was of a legionario in dress uniform, arm in arm with a skeleton wearing a bridal gown. Many legionarios had it tattooed on their arms or chests. The image was iconic, bizarre and strangely brilliant. What's more, it wasn't a disenfranchised biker gang or weird cult that was advocating this out of the ordinary and vaguely occult relationship with death. It was all stamped and sealed with the blessing of those in charge.

That was a good enough reason for me to espouse it all hook, line and sinker.

There was also a very severe and intense spirituality about the Legión. Their coat of arms is a pike crossed with a musket and crossbow, and they often depicted a crucified Christ pinned to it. With my first pay cheque I bought a necklace showing just that, and I wore it with a real sense of pride. Many of their ceremonies revolved around the dying Christ, and although the religion of the Legión was Catholicism, I could see that they had taken it and adjusted it to suit the culture of death they advocated.

The dying Christ was a hero to them, so He became a hero to me. He was prepared to sacrifice Himself for others, as they no doubt hoped they would be able to if called upon to do so. For them there was no greater honour than to die for Spain, Christ and the Legión. As one of their mottos declared, "it is better to die than to be considered a coward".

'El Espíritu De La Muerte,
El Morir En El Combate Es El Mayor Honor, No Se Muere Mas Que Una Vez.
La Muerte Llega Sin Dolor Y El Morir No Es Tan Horrible Como Parece.
Lo Mas Horrible Es Vivir Siendo Un Cobarde.'
'The Spirit of Death,
To die in combat is the highest honour; you can only die once.
Death arrives without pain, and to die is not as awful as it seems.
The most awful thing is to live as a coward.'

As if reinforcing their culture of death, one of their most fabulous and intense rituals is during Holy Week at Easter and their Founder's Day on 20th September, when they parade a life-sized statue of the crucified Christ at all the Legión barracks. Everyone kneels before it and commits themselves anew to the "just cause", which as far as I could tell was Spain, Death and the Legión.

The oxymoron "Viva La Muerte", "Long Live Death", is the most famous of the Legión battle cries; so a dying Christ is exactly the sort of hero they needed. It is a moving ritual to witness, but it has an especially powerful and passionate spiritual significance to all who do take part.

The most famous of all such ceremonies is in Malaga, where a detachment of legionarios parades their holiest statue publicly. You might now understand why this particular statue is called "El Cristo De La Buena Muerte", "The Christ of the Good Death". The event is often televised and serves very successfully to propagate the mystique and reputation of the Legión amongst Spaniards.

Looking back now, I find it amazing that I should have landed in an organisation that seemed to mirror my own desires. I was looking for the truth of God in Christ, and I also wanted and needed adventure, but most of all I had an aching desire to die a "good death", a death that meant something, to me if to no one else. My short troubled life had impressed upon me the fact that the only purpose to life seemed to be death, it was inevitable, and I could not bear the thought of passing out of this life without having something dear to me for which I was prepared to die. Finding the Legión was like coming home. Maybe my "drifting" had been the right choice? Maybe I was destined to be a legionario; to live and die as one?

*

Eventually we were called for our medical. By that time there were about a dozen of us waiting to find out whether we would make it past the doctor's scrutiny. To call it rudimentary would be an understatement - we all passed. I honestly think that we would have had to have been missing a limb or been blind in one eye to have failed.

I had imagined that we would get our uniforms and join our basic training company as soon as being passed fit, but I was to be disappointed. Although the Legión did everything at the double on manoeuvres, the administrative side of military life worked very slowly. I consoled myself with the fact that eventually I was going to be a legionario, and my heart was abuzz with the excitement of it all. At last I was in the middle of a true adventure, one that so far was living up to my expectations.

To top it all, that night I was then reintroduced to an old friend.

To celebrate our passing the medical, we few hopeful legionarios clubbed all our money together to buy a bottle of brandy. Also pulled out by one of the lads was a long strip of hashish, and he started to roll a five-skin joint with the practiced hands of a professional. At first I was hesitant to take part; I did not want anything to jeopardise my chances of enlistment.

The Algerian reassured me.

'The Legión was a Saharan regiment for many decades,' he insisted. 'The whole of Spain knows that it is cultural for legionarios to smoke "chocolate",' as he and the others referred to it. 'It's the NCOs who deal it anyway,' he maintained. 'They control the price and the supply. It's passed down the chain of command from the sergeants and brigadas at the top, to us poor sods at the bottom. It's practically regulated, and as long as you are not caught smoking it everything is fine.'

'What happens if you're caught?' I asked.

'You'll get a thrashing. Paradoxically by those who organised the supply of it in the first place, then after the beating you might get ten or fifteen days Pelotón.'

'Pelotón?' I asked, wondering where I had heard that name before.

'You've probably seen groups of blue boiler suited prisoners running around under armed guard?'

I replied that I had.

'They are called "El Sección de Trabajo", the "Work Section", more often than not referred to as the "Pelotón". It's where the bad boys are sent for punishment.'

'What happens in the Pelotón?' I asked, remembering where I had heard the name before.

The main group of riders in the Tour de France and other road races are often referred to as the "Pelotón".

He raised his right hand and chopped the air while sucking in air through his teeth. Common Legión sign language for a hard time, the same one the driver of the jeep gave when he was describing basic training.

'If you think Legión life is brutal, then compared to the Pelotón it's nursery school. They work twenty hours a day,' he said, 'they are never allowed to sit down, even to eat. They are not allowed to smoke, talk or look any other legionario in the eye. They do everything at the double, and the slightest misdemeanour is punishable by a severe beating. It is very, very hard.' He looked me full in the face. 'You do not want to end up in the Pelotón,' he said. 'Over the years many legionarios have died there.'

I could not imagine a regime so strict and brutal that men died in it, but the Algerian's sincerity convinced me that I should avoid it at all costs. However, even the prospect of the Pelotón did not stop me taking a toke of the joint as it was passed around, and as the familiar kick from the hashish hit my brain, yet another aspect of Legión life won me over.

For the next few days I concentrated on learning as much of the language as I could cram in. I drove the Algerian mad with all my questions, so much so that he threatened to stop helping me. In the end I bribed him with the promise of a few thousand pesetas from my first pay cheque if he continued helping me. It worked, and my Spanish slowly progressed.

*

Eventually we were told that we were going to get our uniforms. Before that happened though, we were taken outside and presented before a brigada; a rank similar to a warrant officer in the British Army. He told us that we had to sign a simple form before we handed over our civilian clothes. I noticed that the form was covered by a sheet of paper hiding everything except the line on which we were supposed to sign.

I looked up at him.

'Is this the contract?' I asked in my very basic Spanish.

He nodded sheepishly.

'How long?' I asked, my heart starting to race.

'Three years,' he replied, with a shrug of his guilty shoulders.

I smiled and signed without a moment's hesitation.

I was in!

I wanted to tell the brigada that all the subterfuge was unnecessary; I was all too willing to sign on the dotted line, wishing only that they had offered me it sooner, but my Spanish was not yet up to such linguistic acrobatics, so I contented myself with a huge grin.

We were then marched away to collect our uniforms, and if you have ever seen films showing how kit is dished out to new recruits, you will be able to imagine what it was like when we were taken to the stores to collect ours. It was mayhem! We were given the eyeball by a sergeant with a tape measure for a brain, who then shouted out instructions to a bunch of lads behind a table. We were ordered to move along the line and the storemen handed out our new kit. It was a conveyor belt. Boots, trousers, shirts, socks, underwear, everything we needed to transform us into legionarios was dropped onto our outstretched arms.

Ordered to strip, our civilian clothes were collected as we scrambled into our new uniforms. I noticed an argument developing amongst the lads behind the table over my Doc Marten boots. They were only a few months old and just beginning to get worn in, my previous pair I had for years and were a prized possession. I let them get on with it. I was climbing into the uniform of the Spanish Foreign Legión, and I could not have been happier.

Some of us swapped trousers that were too short, or jackets that were too tight for ones too large or small on someone else, and eventually, out of the chaos, we were all arrayed in our brand new uniforms. I am sure that I grew six inches in height at that moment. I felt so proud and could not wait to get in front of a mirror so I could make sure that I placed the Chapiri on my head at just the right jaunty angle.

My expectations of joining our basic training company that day were shattered when we were marched back to our temporary accommodation and told that our posting would come through soon.

After a couple of days of maddening frustration on my part, and just before lights out, a sergeant marched into our temporary accommodation. He stood all of us to attention and looked us up and down. He was black, one of the many Africans who join the Spanish Legión as a career and a means to get into Europe legitimately. I was to learn that they had a reputation for sticking to themselves, being good legionarios, and for brutality. This was probably why so many of them made corporal and sergeant. By the expression on this guy's face he didn't look too happy about what he saw before him as he gave us the once over. I cringed inwardly at the latent aggression he exuded. This guy was not to be messed with. I had been around enough men to know which ones to avoid, and he was definitely one!

When done psychologically terrifying us he handed each of us a small brown booklet, issued an order I did not understand and left.

'What was all that about?' I asked the Algerian, when I was certain he had gone.

The Algerian pointed to the book in my hand.

'That,' he said, 'is the Legión Bible. You have to read it, understand it and have most of it memorised before tomorrow morning.'

'Why?' I asked, shaken at the enormity of the command.

'Because that was our new sergeant major, we are going to join his company tomorrow.'

I frantically flicked through the book in my hand. It was all gobbledegook to me.

'What are the most important bits?'

I was desperate to get some of it learnt, but my inability to understand the words I was learning was going to be a severe impediment.

'All of it, but what I would concentrate on if I were you would be the Espíritus.'

I looked up, wondering what the hell he meant. The Algerian took pity on me, and indicated that I should follow him outside.

It was getting dark, and the entire barracks was gathering on the parade ground for the final roll call of the day. It was a sight I loved to watch from the sidelines, not being privileged enough to join in yet.

'Listen,' the Algerian said.

At the end of the small ceremony the officer leading the procedure barked out an order. A second later the whole regiment recited something at the tops of their voices. It was word perfect and sounded reassuringly brutal and brave.

'El Espíritu Del Legionario Es Único Y Sin Igual,
Es De Ciega Y Feroz Acometividad.
De Buscar Siempre Acortar La Distancia Con El Enemigo Y Llegar A
La Bayoneta.'

The Spirit of the Legionario is unique and without equal,
It is one of blind and fierce aggression.
He is always seeking to shorten the distance with the enemy, to finish
with the bayonet.'

'That,' said the Algerian, smiling, 'was the "Espíritu Del Legionario", the "Spirit of the Legionario". Did you know that General Franco was one of the founders of the Legión?'

I nodded: that much I did know.

'Well, the other guy with him was called José Millán-Astray y Terreros, and he wrote the Espíritus. He was a great war hero, wounded many times in battle, he's in the booklet, by the way, and you will be expected to know all about him. If you want to understand the Legión and what it stands for, read and memorise the Espíritus. They sum up the whole ethos and culture of the regiment.'

I looked in my book, finding the one just recited on the parade ground, along with the others Millán-Astray had introduced in the middle of the book. They were not new to me; I had seen these "Espíritus" everywhere. They were normally hand painted on the walls, with the words written on a scroll. I just didn't realise that I would have to know them off by heart as part of my training.

I spent half the night trying to learn the Espíritus, but after struggling for hours I decided that I would concentrate on one. I chose the one I had heard that night, the "Spirit of the Legionario". Some time around three in the morning I was satisfied with my rendition, and hit the sack. Strange how things change, I thought, as the image of the black sergeant's fierce eyes sang me to sleep, a few hours earlier I was looking forward to joining my company, now I was dreading it.

CHAPTER FOUR

The Harsh Reality of the Legión

La Bandera De La Legión,
Es La Mas Gloriosa, Porque Esta Tenida Con La Sangre De Sus
Legionarios.
The Flag of the Legión,
Is the most glorious, because it is stained with the blood of her
Legionarios.

Early the next morning, after the usual breakfast of coffee, bread and chorizo, we waited apprehensively for our call up to the training company. It came mid-morning, and I breathed a sigh of relief when a young, cheerful and fresh-faced lance corporal turned up to collect us.

The first thing on the menu when we turned up at our new company HQ was to be allocated a bunk. Mine was one hundred and eighty-five, and once again the Legión code of austerity drove itself home as I looked around me. The company building was nothing more than a corrugated cowshed lined with double bunks. There were no lockers, apart from ones at a small part at the bottom of the hut that was crudely sectioned off with wooden screens, and home to the company lance corporals. It seemed as if we were going to have to live out of our kitbags. With growing apprehension I then looked at the bedding. It looked like we only got one sheet and one blanket each. Where we had just come from there were not the draughts we had here, plus we had two sheets and four blankets, and we were still cold at night. I shivered involuntarily.

Leaving our kitbags next to our bunks we were ordered outside and given our first introduction to the basics of soldiering.

How to salute was followed by "attention" and "at ease" orders. These we mastered reasonably quickly and we immediately started to feel like soldiers. That was until we were introduced to marching, Legión-style. It was unbelievably fast, so fast that I wanted to break into a run merely to keep up. I was informed by the other guys when we were given a cigarette break that groin strains were common amongst new recruits, and I was beginning to understand why.

There were three different marches we were going to have to learn. The one we had just been doing at breakneck speed that felt impossible to master, a slow ceremonial march somewhat like a slow goose-step, and then there was the "Paso Ligero". This was more of a run than a march. In this one the gun was held at a forty-five degree angle across the chest and the knees were expected to come up to waist height as you ran. Not having a gun at this time we had to tuck our thumbs into our belts to do it, which made it even harder. Each march had its technical difficulty, and all were going to be hard to master, but the fast march was by far and away the hardest.

A few hours into our training, and just when I was starting to get to terms with the speed at which we were expected to march, along with the various orders in Spanish that came with it, the black sergeant made an appearance. Called to attention, we waited apprehensively as our good-natured lance corporal was called over and asked how we were getting on. Listening attentively, the sergeant nodded a few times as he watched us over the corporal's shoulder.

My heart was beating like a drum as they both then made their way over to us. The sergeant's face was implacable as he walked up and down the line, stopping to look at each one of us closely. Legión protocol dictated that when at attention you kept your head and chin up, and that you never looked an NCO or officer in the eye when spoken to.

It was my misfortune that he stopped in front of me and asked me a question. Not having a clue about what was being asked of me, I decided the best option was to keep silent, probably not the best decision I was to make that day. The lightning-fast rabbit punch to my solar plexus floored me, leaving me gasping for breath and wondering how a man could hit me so hard without appearing to move. Having been prepared by the Algerian as to what could be expected if I incurred the wrath of the NCOs, I was half-expecting the punch, but nothing fully prepares you for the pain, so it was still a terrible shock to the system.

I also knew that I was expected to get up onto my feet and back to attention as quickly as possible. This I did as I wondered how I was going to avoid getting hit again. Once I was up the sergeant asked me the same question, only this time I thought I heard something I knew in his question. It was his African accent that had thrown me first time. Now I was pretty certain he was asking me to recite the Spirit of the Legionario.

I threw caution to the wind, and without knowing for certain that I was doing the right thing, I recited the motto, stumbling only once or twice with a few words.

'Are you English?' the sergeant asked me in English, his face breaking into a sudden smile.

'Yes, sergeant,' I replied, confused by this sudden reversal of fortune and the fact that I was being addressed in my native tongue.

'When did you learn the Espíritu?' he asked.

'Last night, sergeant,' I replied, hoping he would not ask for another one, considering the fact that the one I had just recited was the only one I knew.

'That was well remembered. Do you know any more?'

I shook my head, praying that my honesty would not land me in too much trouble.

'No, sergeant. I learnt that one last night. I thought I would try to learn one every day.'

'You do that, English boy,' the sergeant said, smiling, 'and I will come and see you every day to make sure that you do.'

With that he passed down the line, stopping a few legionarios down. A quick question was followed just as quickly by another rabbit punch into the stomach of the hapless victim who was unable to answer satisfactorily whatever it was he had been asked.

So came about our first introduction to Legión life, and only then, in the full light of day, was the mystique of the Legión starting to take on a very different and painful phase. One that we were going to have to come to terms with sooner rather than later.

One thing I quickly learnt, and something that will sound strange to you, is that there was no animosity involved in Legión beatings. It was a cultural tradition and hardly ever personal. It was true that a sergeant or corporal could slap you around the face, or punch you in the stomach for a minor infraction of the rules. They could even mete out a severe beating for something more serious, which would leave the victim bruised or needing stitches, but it was important to understand that this was because they had the authority to do so; and also because that was how you were punished in the Legión. It was tradition. Millán-Astray wanted legionarios to be some of the hardest soldiers on the planet, and he decided that you didn't do that by treating them with kid gloves.

The punishments hurt, of course they hurt; they were meant to. As far as I could tell though, the most important thing was that you accepted the reprimand for what it was, improved on whatever it was that had initiated the warning, and got on with your soldiering.

My English sensibility took some time to get used to this, until I finally realised that it meant no more than a verbal reprimand would have in the British Army. We were soldiers; we were being trained to kill. Discipline had to be hard and intense. The Legión was the spearhead rapid reaction force of the Spanish Army, first in and last out. Culturally we prided ourselves on the fact that we were constantly ready for battle. What good would we be if our training had not prepared us for the reality of war?

I bore the training philosophically. I had come to them after all. No one had forced me to sign on; I was a willing volunteer.

Only once during my training did I find this sort of punishment taking on a personal aspect.

The basic training company I was in, like all the others, used recently promoted lance corporals to run things. A lance corporal differed greatly from a full corporal in authority. In normal Legión life they were not allowed to administer beatings, actually they were often the brunt of discipline if their particular section was not up to speed, but in basic training they were given more responsibility for discipline, and were, therefore, allowed to hand out mild slaps or punches.

Only a few days into training I discovered that our company had one particular lance corporal who was especially vicious, taking a perverse delight in handing out as much physical punishment as he could to those beneath him.

It is hard to describe how a punch in the stomach, or a full on slap around the face from an eighteen-stone soldier could be administered in a compassionate or sympathetic way. It sounds like a contradiction, yet that was often the case. You had done something wrong that had crossed the line, and you had received your chastisement. The strange thing was that often the same lance corporal who had hit you would be handing out cigarettes or even inviting you to share a joint an hour or two later.

The particular lance corporal I mention here was different in his approach. He wanted to hurt, and by his face you knew that he was taking a peculiar delight in inflicting pain. He was popular amongst his fellow lance corporals, but he was universally hated by us recruits.

One day he disappeared, and rumour had it that he was in the Pelotón up at the main barracks, not as a guard, but as a prisoner, and no one seemed to know why.

A few weeks later a very strange thing happened. After supper one night, we made our way back to our company building to be greeted by the black sergeant and some other company corporals with a visitor. To our surprise we saw that it was our sadistic former lance corporal still in his blue prison boiler suit.

Once we were all inside the sergeant informed us that we had a couple of minutes, and left with the other NCOs. It took only a few seconds for the reality of the situation to dawn on everyone present, and for the prisoner concerned to realise that he was in for the beating of his life. I did not join in; not because I did not want to, but because I was not sure why the guy was getting such a serious going over. I decided that the best thing was to hang back and watch, although I must admit that I did take great delight in watching him getting pounded by a baying mob of recruits who were only too happy to give back a little bit of what he had previously been dishing out. I never did find out what he had done, but it must have been serious to warrant such a violent punishment.

*

I had other things on my mind anyway, like coping physically. Getting fit enough to keep up was hard at first, but gradually I settled into the routine of training. As my lungs and body got used to being at full stretch from sun up to sun down, I came to love it. From not being able to run a kilometre without stopping halfway around because I was out of breath, to being able to finish an eight-kilometre run in less than forty minutes in the space of a few weeks was no mean achievement. I became leaner, fitter and meaner, and was growing in confidence every single day.

Not everything went my way to start off with.

I was the only foreigner in my particular company, and because of this I was something of an oddity to the Spanish lads. For the most part they were poorly educated working class, with not a single decent English-speaker amongst them, apart from the Algerian. Most accepted me, taking me under their wing and guiding me through a change in lifestyle that was hard enough for them never mind someone who couldn't speak the lingo. Some others though, decided that my Englishness, along with my inability to speak Spanish, was good material for a laugh.

At first it started off with a few coming up to me and saying in very heavily accented Spanish:

'Do you speak English?'

When I replied that I did, they would laugh and walk off. Within a few days it was happening all the time and I realised that I was becoming the butt of a joke that was getting out of control. One night, after lights out as I was lying shivering in bed trying to keep warm, I realised that I was going to have to take matters into my own hands.

Next morning, after breakfast, and just before roll call, I waited. First one guy came up and asked me if I spoke English, then another. I ignored them; I was waiting for one or two people in particular. Just as we were falling in my moment came. The largest legionario in the company came up, and with a sly grin to his mates he opened his mouth to speak. He was a big lad, well over six foot, a bodybuilder who was keen to get in the "Grupo de Operaciones Especiales", the Special Forces unit of the Legión, and as soon as he started to say "do you..." I punched him as hard as I could in the face.

The reason I waited was because he was one of the recognised hard men of the company. Flooring a tiny guy would not have had the effect I wanted. I had to make a serious statement if I wanted this to work.

He hit the deck with a stunned thud.

I must explain here that, although shouting matches were common amongst legionarios, punch-ups were not. Unlike in Britain where things can quickly turn physically violent, in Spain they are more vocal in sorting out arguments. In my whole time in the Legión I only ever saw a few fights between legionarios. I doubt the same could be said in the British Army.

I was relying on the fact that I had floored a big man to reinforce my statement, and so far the plan was working. I had also been practising what I would say when I had everyone's attention, by using a Spanish-English dictionary one of the lads on home leave had brought back for me. In hesitant and badly accented Spanish, I then explained to the astonished and strangely silent company that I was tired of being the brunt of the joke, and I would give the next man who came up to me to take the mickey exactly the same as I had just dished out to the guy lying on the floor. By this time the bodybuilder had got to his feet. I told him that if he wanted redress I would meet him wherever and whenever he wanted. Still shocked he merely nodded and walked off, rubbing his chin.

With a sick tightening in the stomach I suddenly noticed the black sergeant watching from the sidelines. My heart sank and skipped a beat. What I had done was wrong, and I wondered whether I would end up with a beating, or in Pelotón. Strangely nothing happened until after the roll call had been taken, but as expected, I was eventually called to one side by the sergeant, who took me into the company building. My heart was in my mouth at the thought of what might shortly be dished out, but instead of chastising me for what had happened outside, he showed me a piece of paper he had in his hand.

'Did you know that you were eligible for a weekend pass?' he asked, his face rigid and implacable, so much so that I could not tell what he was thinking at all.

I shook my head, confused as to why he had not mentioned me punching the bodybuilder.

'That's because as soon as I put this on the noticeboard it's filled in within five minutes,' he explained. 'Competition is rife, and we only give them to those we think deserve them.'

He handed me a pen.

I was staggered at this reversal of fortune, and pleased that the sergeant had realised that what I had done earlier was justifiable and necessary. I was receiving a silent tacit approval, and inwardly I breathed a huge sigh of relief.

'But I've got nowhere to go,' I replied.

'Malaga's a decent place for a weekend pass,' he answered, with what might have been interpreted as a smile.

I smiled back, thanked him and wrote my name at the top of the list.

*

I took the sergeant's advice and bought a train ticket to Malaga. It was six o'clock on Friday evening when I walked out of the barracks, and I was not expected back until 9 p.m. on Sunday.

I had just been paid, so the fact that I had nowhere to go didn't bother me too much. After wandering around Malaga for a while, I bought a couple of nights in a swanky hotel. Because of my uniform they nearly refused me a room until they saw the money in my hand. Once inside, I had a long hot bath then went out for a beer.

It was an eventful night. I became a minor celebrity in my uniform and attracted a lot of attention. I had a few drinks bought me by some Spaniards who still thought that Franco was the greatest leader Spain had ever had, and some more by some English tourists who had never heard of the Spanish Legión and were surprised at finding out there was one. Later I was threatened with a knife by a Moroccan, who told me that his grandfather had been murdered by the Legión in the Ifni War in 1957-58.

It happened in the early hours of the morning in a backstreet bar playing Flamenco on an old juke box, and everyone present froze as the young Moroccan pulled out a very large flick knife. I was extremely drunk by this time, but not too drunk to realise that I was mere moments from having to fight for my life. The way the knife had swiftly appeared, and the way he held it left me in no doubt that this guy was no stranger to knife fights. I also had a knife down the side of my boot, but even in my inebriated state I knew that pulling it would have escalated the confrontation.

Feeling strangely calm and confident in my new uniform, I told him that although I was a legionario, I personally had nothing to do with his grandfather's death, and that currently the Legión was not at war with him or his country, so there was no need to bear grudges about something that had happened so many years ago.

In a fit of macho bravado, no doubt inspired by my new found confidence and regimental pride, I then said that although there was no need to be enemies today, tomorrow might be different. I also assured him that I would do whatever was necessary if ordered to, as I was sure he would in defence of his country. I was unsure how this last bit would go down with him, but I was determined to let him know that although I did not want to fight him, I was not afraid of doing so.

He thought over what I said for a while, then smiled and bought me a brandy as the knife mysteriously disappeared as fast as it had been produced. The bar breathed a sigh of relief and the Flamenco started up again.

The sun was rising when I made my way back to the hotel, where I slept for twenty-four hours straight, right through until mid-morning on Sunday.

*

On the train I felt excited to be going back even though I was unsure at what reaction I would receive after flooring the bodybuilder. Maybe he had had time to think about what had happened and decided that he did want a rematch after all? As I walked in through the white arch and past the sentry, a few groups huddled together having a smoke shouted out greetings, and I was invited over for a beer by others.

It seemed that the company had talked about nothing else since my incident with the bodybuilder, and that in my absence everyone had decided that I was "loco" – "crazy". This was said as a compliment and came with a smile and a slap on the back. There was no doubt about it, my social standing had improved and I was certainly treated with a lot more respect than previously. With a sigh of relief I realised that I was now fully accepted as one of them, even if they did think I was a little bit crazy.

One lad to get alongside me was called Pedro. His swarthy looks and dark disposition led me to believe that there was some gypsy blood in him, but asking whether there was could have led to a severe argument. The Spanish seemed to hate and respect the gypsies in equal measure, and accusing a non-gypsy of being one would have been a serious faux pas. He did tell me that he was from Barcelona and that he was here because he was on the run from the police. I asked him what for, but he merely put his finger to his lips and shook his head.

He was quiet and slightly mysterious, and like me he had a reputation as a "loco" after waking a fellow recruit up in the middle of the night with a knife at his throat. Apparently something had been said about his mother to which he had taken exception. Needless to say, the insult was never repeated and afterwards Pedro was treated with a great deal of respect. Maybe that was why he identified with what I did.

'Sticking together,' he said, 'we can deal with anyone who gives us a hard time.'

He then pulled his finger slowly across his throat and smiled.

Although not keen to actually kill anyone who disrespected me, I decided that having Pedro on my side was no bad thing. The two of us together were enough to put off anyone who tried to give us a hard time. After first spitting on our hands and then shaking them, we swore a "Legión Jura", an oath of friendship to each other.

El Espíritu de Amistad,
De Juramento Entre Cada Dos Hombres.
The Spirit of Friendship;
A sacred oath made between two men.

This was no small thing to do and I took it very seriously. There was a sincerity and permanence to it, and although I have not seen Pedro for over twenty-four years, I still consider the oath to be real. I think about him and pray for him often, and hope that I might see him again one day, so that we can continue our friendship.

Pleased at this development, I passed around some English cigarettes I had bought in Malaga, and as a joint was rolled I realised that for the first time in many years I was starting to feel at home.

*

As the weeks passed our training started to take on a more serious tone. The runs became harder, the square-bashing longer and more intense, and the NCOs more vicious in their disciplining of misdemeanours. It was all for a purpose, to squeeze out of us the mental weakness that was holding us back, and to fashion us into men who would not hesitate to kill. We were being moulded into legionarios, and no one was going to get through unless they had been shaped correctly.

There were many punishments meted out for those of us who did not give as much as those training us thought was enough. As well as the obligatory slaps around the face and punches to the stomach, there were others, common to every soldier's basic training experience;

such as standing squats, push-ups and taking in a few circuits of the parade ground as the rest of the company not singled out for a "beasting" enjoyed a smoke and a breather.

All such punishments were designed to develop mental strength and physical endurance, and all succeeded in proving to us that the human body is capable of far more than it thinks it is if it is pushed hard enough. I became amazed at what I was capable of, and quickly started to revel in my new found fitness.

There was one particular punishment we all hated with a vengeance and dreaded above all others. It was euphemistically called "El Montana De La Muerte", "The Hill of Death". It was less of a mountain and more of a hill, some one hundred metres from the base to the top. Maybe not the longest run in the world, but it was rock strewn and very steep, having a perilous thirty to forty degree incline. Being ordered to run up and down it while doing the "Paso Ligero" and maintaining perfect rank and file was not easy, in fact it was impossible, but I now realise that that was the whole object of the punishment. Doing something almost impossible and getting it right eventually makes the hard easy.

Tempers flared, and fights often broke out as we were forced up and down the hill time and time again. I must confess to once smacking the lad in front of me with my rifle butt in the back of the head because he was causing me to lose my step by dropping back on my feet. He was carted off to the infirmary for stitches, but at least the sergeant clouting me around the head because I was not in step left me alone after that.

Many were sick as the intensity of the workout burnt us up; some even passing out and getting stomped on until they were dragged out of the column as the rest of us were ordered to regroup and maintain file. You couldn't think for trying to breathe, and stars flashed before your eyes as your body tried to collect enough oxygen to function. Sweat ran off you like water, and every time you got to the bottom you prayed that you would not be turned around and ordered back up. You were though, many more times than you thought possible, until eventually, right when you thought that your lungs were going to burst and your boots were too full of lead to lift any more, the order would be given to halt.

Those moments, as your aching body fell to its knees and you threw up on the ground, and similar events as we trained to the edge of endurance, were the moments when you realised that the Legión uniform was not easily won. They were the moments when you wondered whether you would manage to stay the course, and they were when you realised that the myth and stature of the Legión could not be owned by those without the determination to succeed.

Thankfully though, I was determined enough, and although many dropped out and were sent home, I wasn't. No one could have been happier than me when in mid-December we were informed that the passing out parade was going to take place in early January.

First though, I was going to have my first Spanish Christmas.

*

The Spanish love Christmas. As well as the deep religious significance it holds to what is a very Catholic country, culturally it is something the Spanish embrace wholeheartedly. It becomes a fiesta of grand proportions. What I was not expecting was how it would affect us in the Legión. Everyone started to get into the festive spirit, and I grew increasingly surprised at how lax discipline became in the few days leading up to the holiday. Everyone seemed to switch off, so I decided that the best thing to do was to roll with it, determining that a few days' rest and recuperation would not do me any harm at all.

Food is something the Spanish are also very keen on, and I grew to love the Mediterranean diet. Chorizo, tortillas, salad with olive oil and vinegar, and of course paella, all became firm favourites. As did the Legión's favourite meal, a dish of meat, potato and lentils served up with mountains of bread, salad and gut rot wine that you had to dilute with water just to make it drinkable.

At Christmas I came across something special.

It was called "Turrón", a sweet popular at this time of year. It is made of almonds, honey and marzipan. It came in various guises, and I had great fun trying them all. It is still a firm favourite of mine.

There are two basic types of Turrón, soft Jijona sometimes known as Turrón Blando, which is smooth and has the consistency of peanut butter, and hard Alicante, sometimes known as Turrón Duro, which is like a thick almond nougat candy, similar in consistency to peanut brittle. As well as these there are various other types including a chocolate one. My favourite was the soft Jijona, and I could sit down and eat a whole bar in one sitting. It was gorgeous.

That Christmas Eve, with a lot of the company away on home leave, I was invited to go to a local village with a few friends on a day pass. We caught the train and had a leisurely day in a beautiful Andalucían village perched high in the mountains. It was a picturesque place, with traditional whitewashed houses and streets almost as steep as the Montana Del Muerte back at the camp. We had a few beers in a small bar, and egg and chips along with a bottle or two of local wine in a widow's kitchen that served as the village's cheap restaurant.

Needless to say we were pretty chilled-out, and didn't even take offence as the few young girls that were around were swiftly dragged indoors by their parents. It appeared that the Legión was not loved by everyone.

Only later did I come to learn the reason for this. The Legión had apparently earned itself a fearsome and brutal reputation during the Spanish Civil War, and previously in the African colonial wars. Along with the Arab Regulares (Moroccan tribesmen recruited by the Spanish as a force to help them develop a North African Empire, and famous for being able to traverse "dead ground" unseen and unheard), the Legión were the spearhead shock troops of the Civil War.

In the early months of the war General Franco used the fact that the Legión were professional and seasoned troops to great advantage against the mainly unprofessional volunteers of the Republican Government. Many towns and families who supported the Republican cause have horror stories about the atrocities committed by the Nationalist Army during this particularly vicious conflict, and afterwards as Franco consolidated his dictatorship.

Apparently the whole male population from fourteen years of age to seventy in towns captured, who had put up resistance were often shot out of hand. Sometimes to save bullets they even had their throats slit. The regulares often had to be stopped taking the genitalia of those they had killed as war trophies, so it was not surprising that most parents locked up their daughters whenever they saw the olive green uniform and trademark Chapiri.

All this was unknown to me then, but after having had a great day, and as the sun started to set, we made our way back to the train station, only to be told that when checking the return timetable we had not looked to see whether the trains ran on a holiday. To our distress we realised that we had missed the last train back, and we were twelve miles by road from the camp with only one and a half hours until evening roll call. Unfortunately we had also spent all our money, so a taxi was out of the question.

There was nothing else for it; we were going to have to run back.

There were five of us, and amazingly one of the lads suggested running across country, stating that it was only eight miles as the crow flies. I didn't agree. It was already getting dark, we did not know the ground, and there were some amazing cliffs and sheer drops in that part of the world that I didn't fancy coming face to face with in the pitch dark. The road was a no-brainer as far as I was concerned; according to the locals it ran straight to the barracks, so there was no possibility of taking a wrong turn.

Unfortunately I was the only one who agreed, so as the other four set off across the countryside, I tucked my Chapiri into my belt, tightened up my boots and set off down the road. It was a hard run, some of the hills were huge, and after close to one hour and twenty minutes of solid running, with roll call only ten minutes off, I wondered whether I had made the wrong decision. Being late for roll call was potentially a Pelotón offence, so I gritted my teeth and pushed my tired legs harder. Fortunately, as the minute hand of my watch crept up to the hour, the barracks came into view. With only seconds to spare I fell in and gasped a tired "presente" when my name was called.

The amazing thing is that two months before I could not have run one mile without stopping for a breather, and just now I had finished twelve up and down some horrendous hills in heavy boots with a belly full of wine and chips in only an hour and a half, so naturally I felt justifiably pleased with myself.

That night there was a load of free food and drink laid on for us in the company hut. The party lasted all night with general drunkenness and debauchery being the order of the day. It was obviously going to be impossible to sleep, so I collared myself a bottle of decent wine, some hashish and a bar of Turrón; I then found myself a quiet spot at the back of the hut and tried to enjoy this crazy version of Christmas.

The next morning the hut looked like a whirlwind had passed through it. There were bodies lying everywhere, some of them in pools of vomit. I looked around for the lads I had gone to the village with. They were not there, so I asked around. Apparently they had turned up at three in the morning having got hopelessly lost. After being given a slap or two by the sergeant on guard, they were ordered onto the parade ground first thing in the morning for a few hours of extensive drill. This was followed by a beasting up and down the Montana De La Muerte. Not the best way to spend your Christmas Day.

Meanwhile, having the day off and with nothing else to do, I had a few beers and a joint. After a fine Christmas lunch that included another bottle of decent wine, I then fell asleep under an almond tree in the time honoured tradition of the siesta.

God alone knew what New Year was going to be like!

All in all though, my life was looking good. I felt as if I had had a complete reversal of fortune since waking up on that beach in Marbella. From being down and out a couple of months ago with nothing and no one to belong to, I was now on my way to becoming a fully fledged legionario, a member of the Spanish Army's elite, a soldier of fortune owing my allegiance for the next three years to Legión and to Spain. I was living a real life adventure straight out of a book I might have read as a kid.

Maybe I had found my calling. I was happy enough. So much so that if someone had come up to me at that exact moment and said that this is it, this is what you will be doing for the next thirty years of your life, I would have snapped their hands off. I loved being a soldier. I loved the fact that I knew exactly what was expected of me. From morning to night I felt like the cat that had got the cream, and to top it all, I was actually proving to be quite good at it!

CHAPTER FIVE

Dangerous Hashish

Todos Los Hombres Legionarios Son Bravos;
Cada Nación Tiene Fama De Bravura;
Aquí es Preciso Demonstrar Que Pueblo es el Mas Valiente.
All legionarios are brave;
And every nation is renowned for its bravery;
Here it is necessary to demonstrate which country is the bravest.

The passing out parade was not quite what I expected. It was laid back when I had been expecting something a bit more intense. I enjoyed it though. We marched, we sang the Legión hymn, we shouted out a few of the Espíritus, and when the colonel stated that we had passed out and we were all fully fledged legionarios we all shouted:

'Viva Espana! Viva la Legión!'

We threw our Chapiris up into the air to celebrate then we all went and got blind drunk.

*

The next morning, I was informed by one of the lieutenants that there was another ceremony I was yet to undergo where I would be expected to "Jura de Bandera", "Take the Oath of Allegiance to the Flag", and that this would take place at the regiment I was posted to.

Later I asked Pedro what this was all about. He said that it was exactly what it said; you kissed the flag publicly in front of witnesses, thereby pledging your oath to Spain and the Legión.

I merely shrugged.

I was a fully signed up and sealed legionario, I had signed a contract as a soldier of fortune to the Spanish Government, and for the next three years my soul was theirs - if they wanted me to kiss the Spanish flag then I would.

Pedro then asked me why I had joined the Spanish Army and not the British.

'Do you not love your country?' he asked.

I laughed and showed him again the Union Jack tattoos I had on my arm and chest.

'No, Pedro,' I said, 'I love my country. I always have and I always will, but for the moment, until that contract runs out, I am a legionario.'

'But what if we have to fight the English in a war?' he asked with a mischievous grin.

I shrugged again.

'Then I will try to do my duty as a legionario,' I replied, with slightly false bravado as I wondered inwardly whether I could kill a fellow countryman if it came to it.

What I did not explain to him was that kissing the Spanish flag, or fighting for Spain was not anything that threatened my nationality as an Englishman. All I wanted was adventure.

As a boy back home I had been weaned on stories like Beau Geste, where three brothers famously ran off to join the French Foreign Legion rather than face dishonour at home. As a child I had idolised men like Clive of India who, long before the British Raj came into being, was a mercenary in the East India Company that sold its services to whichever maharaja paid them enough and paved the way for the British Raj.

I was a proud member of a nation that had produced men like Drake, Wellington, Nelson, General Gordon and Churchill, and I was then, and still am now, intensely proud of what my small nation is and stands for. As far as I was concerned I was merely another in a long line of Englishmen looking for something to do in a world that had otherwise gone sterile on him.

Joining the British Army was something I was not adverse to, but where was the fun in that? I was looking for something extraordinary; I was looking for an adventure that would define me as a person for the rest of my life. I wanted to know that I was alive, that I had done something of value with the few allotted years I was allowed on this planet earth.

What is life without risk anyway?

I had seen the mundane, and it was nowhere I wanted to live. As far as I was concerned, only a life lived to the full was a life worth living.

*

A few days later they asked each one of us where we would like to be posted. There were four choices: The main barracks in Ronda here in Spain, Ceuta or Melilla, Spanish enclaves on the North African Coast, or Fuerteventura in the Canary Islands.

The only one that appealed to me was Fuerteventura, firstly because I had been to the Canaries when I was in the Merchant Navy, and also because I had been speaking to a Polish guy the previous night in the bar, who had just finished a tour of duty out there. He said that it was a tough regiment, but the weather was good all year around, unlike Ronda, which froze in winter and baked in summer, or North Africa that baked even worse during the day before plummeting to almost zero in the desert every night.

He also talked about the small resort in the north of the island called Corralejo, where female German and Scandinavian tourists came with the express intention of getting it on with the legionarios. He made it sound like they were lining up, so naturally I put my name down for Fuerteventura, reasoning that one place was a good as another unless there were blonde Swedish tourists looking for a good time to tip the balance in its favour.

Until the postings came through, and to prepare us for our regiment, we underwent some more training. This included weapons training, armed and unarmed self-defence, and some more intense battlefield tactics.

Our standard issue weapon was the Fusil de Asalto CETME, a 7.62mm semi-automatic assault rifle, accurate up to eight hundred metres if you were a good shot, five hundred if you were average. It was a sturdy weapon, and as far as I could tell you could drive a tank over it and it would still fire. It weighed 3.5kg, so it was not light, but because of its heavy wooden stock it was a handy weapon when you got up close and personal, a type of combat on which the Legión prided itself. We also practised with the Star Machine Gun and Automatic Pistol that were standard Spanish Army issue. There was also limited training with hand grenades, mortars and heavy machine guns, because these were kit we would receive more detailed training on when we finally got posted to our companies.

However, when we underwent our tactical battlefield training I started to realise that the Legión was hopelessly outdated. Unlike the British Army that had fought in nearly every conflict since the end of the Second World War, the Spanish had done nothing since the Ifni War of 1957-58. This and its self-imposed exile from NATO by Franco during his rule meant that its fighting force was not up to date in modern warfare techniques. It would probably be true to say that it was desperately old-fashioned

The interrogation techniques we were taught also confirmed the fact that the Legión was still living in a world where war crimes did not exist.

'If you have three prisoners,' a huge sergeant brought in to teach us said as he forced three legionarios to kneel on the floor before him, 'and you need information from them quickly because your friends are being killed…' He pulled his pistol from its holster and put it to the first legionario's head. 'You shoot the first one in the head without even asking him a question... Bang!' he shouted as he put his boot in the surprised lad's back and pushed him to the floor. 'The next one along in the line you ask the question of. I can guarantee that he will start speaking, but if for any reason he decides to be a hero, you shoot him if he does not answer your first question within five seconds... Bang!' He shouted again as he pushed the second one into the dust. 'The third one will answer, but if he doesn't, you get the information out of him by any means possible.'

He then went on to demonstrate what any means possible meant. It involved garrotting until they passed out, and when they woke up, garrotting them again if they still did not talk.

'A particularly nasty technique,' he said with a smile. 'It's like dying many times over only to come back to life seeing me with the rope standing over you waiting to do it all again.'

You broke fingers, half-drowned the poor sods, even snapping elbows and knees, although pressure points seemed to be this sergeant's particular passion as he demonstrated enthusiastically on some of us. I was amazed at the amount of pain that could be inflicted merely by bending or pushing a part of the anatomy here and there with very little force.

I hate to say anything disrespectful about the Legión, so please don't get me wrong; if sheer blood, guts and ferocity had anything to do with it, the Legión was second to no other fighting force on the planet. One-on-one, toe-to-toe, I would not like to put money on anyone else, but macho blood and guts heroics is not all that goes to making a successful armed unit. What does is up-to-date weapons, kit and training, and as far as I could tell the Legión had precious few of any of them.

I was shown a booklet by a corporal about this time, which disclosed how much money was spent on the average Spanish soldier compared to the average British one. The figures were startling; statistically the British Army spent forty times more on each soldier. This might be slightly misrepresentative because Spain still had conscription when I was there (although the Legión only accepted volunteers, and probably got the lion's share of money), but the quality of weapons and support offered were obviously inadequate.

*

Note: I understand from my recent research that the Legión is now up to date and recognised as a very professional fighting unit amongst

European land forces. Spain is now a member of NATO, and the Legión fought with distinction in the first Iraq War, it has also seen duty during the Bosnian conflict, something I am sure of which they are very proud. This was all after my time though, and it would not be unfair to say that the army I had joined in 1982 had changed little in the previous forty years.

*

Apart from the quite old-fashioned training we received, some of the other things that happened during training were very strange, and served to tell their own story about how much the Legión still lived in the past, relying on blind obedience and bloody-minded determination to get it through whatever situation it got itself into.

One happened the day after we had seen a war movie on the television in the bar. The picture showed German soldiers leaping out of moving trucks, and as we watched them tumbling out there was a collective groan of disappointment from those watching the film.

I asked one of the lads next to me why everyone had demonstrated such emotion, he laughed.

'Our colonel is a complete nutter,' he replied. 'He is famous for putting into action anything he sees on the television. I can virtually guarantee that tomorrow we will all be jumping out of moving trucks.'

Sure enough, after roll call, we were lined up and ordered into the back of trucks that then proceeded to roll around the camp as we jumped out. It would have been hilarious if there had not been so many injuries. In my lorry, instead of telling us to jump one by one, our sergeant threw us all out in one big heap.

We ended up as a disjointed pile of broken legionarios on the tarmac. More than a couple found teeth missing after getting a gun barrel in the mouth; others suffered various knocks and bumps, including a broken ankle as one lad landed awkwardly on another soldier. Eventually though, we got the hang of it, and became quite proficient at leaping out and taking up smart defensive positions as the truck sped on at thirty kilometres an hour.

On another occasion we were lined up as a company and ordered to run and jump off a ledge in front of us into a dry river bottom. The edge was ten metres ahead of us, and we had no idea how deep the drop was or what we could expect at the bottom when we landed. It was a test of obedience, and the lieutenant supervising proceedings casually explained to us that a legionario did as he was ordered without arguing. So after reciting the "Espíritu de Disciplina", "The Spirit of Obedience", to a man we ran and jumped.

El Espíritu De Disciplina,

Cumplirá Su Deber, Obedecerá Hasta Morir.
The Spirit of Discipline,
Fulfil Your Duty, Obey unto Death.

I still remember the shock of the unknown as I leapt into the air, praying that wherever I landed was not going to hurt too much. It was a horrendous drop of ten to twelve feet with nothing but boulders and sharply formed ruts at the bottom. We had previously been shown how to jump and land by bending our legs to cushion the landing, and using the stock of our gun to break the fall. That way we maintained contact with our gun and were ready to use it as soon as we landed. I did this and thankfully managed to miss any obstacles, but there were injuries amongst some others, mainly broken legs and twisted ankles. I wondered at the logic of putting out of action good men in what was merely a test of obedience, but I enjoyed it nevertheless.

Once we were even ordered to run as hard as we could at a brick wall. Anyone thought to be not hitting it with enough force was ordered to do it again. I realised that the best way to hit it was with a side-on combined shoulder and thigh, but it still hurt like hell, and the bruises were astonishing the day after.

Mindless, you might think, but gradually I came to realise that things were changing in me. Where once I would have wondered why some idiot was asking me to do something merely to prove a point, and then done it with reservation in my mind if forced to, I came to obey without questioning whatever it was I was told to do. I became not so much an automaton, as someone who willingly did what he was told because he wanted to, and because that was what was expected.

I was paid to soldier, to obey my orders. That was what I had signed up for. I could not undo what I had done, nor did I want to. I suppose I found comfort in the fact that the rules defining my life were clear. There was no ambiguity in what was expected of me, no freedom to mismanage my own life. I was dependent on others for my welfare, and a part of me found great solace in that. Under my own guidance my life had been going nowhere; evidence of such was the mess I was in prior to joining up. I had willingly handed myself over to the Legión lock, stock and barrel because that was the easiest path to take; and now I was no longer my own man - the Legión owned me.

The downside was that after such indoctrination, if I had been asked to pick up a gun, fix a bayonet and kill someone, soldier or civilian, I would have done it. It was not the order itself that became important to me, or the right or wrong in it; it was merely the fulfilling of it that mattered. I was judged on my compliance and my willingness to obey, and in me they found a willing pupil. This was reflected in the way I was increasingly respected and liked by my fellow legionarios and those in command over me.

Understanding and observing the subtle changes in me, I started to understand how the Legión could have been responsible for such outstanding feats of bravery during battle; and there are no shortages of proof of their valour under fire. They have always been some of the bravest men ever to wear a Spanish uniform, but there is also the alter ego to such a means of programming, the flip side to the coin that has haunted the Legión's history. Such as the cold-blooded murder of Arab civilians during their wars in Africa, or the execution of captured prisoners of war without trial during the Spanish Civil War.

There was no shortage of war crimes during the Civil War, with both sides committing some obscene acts of brutality and murder. The Republicans, who were almost universally supported by the democratic West's media propaganda, and because they were fighting what was euphemistically termed a "romantic" war, have not been as badly vilified by modern historians as the Nationalists, who suffered from Franco's associations with, and support from, Nazi Germany and Fascist Italy. If you read the books that tell it like it was, you will find that no one conducted themselves righteously during the battle for Spain's soul.

Many condemn the Legión and its men for its bloodthirsty ways in the wars it had fought in, and not without reason, but the strangest thing for me to admit to now is that I would have been no different myself. I was now a soldier, and not just any soldier either, I was a legionario, and I knew that if I was asked to kill, I would kill. Of this fact there is no shadow of a doubt in my mind. I had become a trained killer, someone capable of taking another human being's life merely because he had been ordered to do so.

Yet the most intriguing and disturbing thing for me to confess and come to terms with is that I was proud of whom I had become. I had withstood the fire of refining, and now stood tall and proud as a member of one of the most brutal regiments in the Western world. I had earned the right to sing the songs and wear the uniform; and no one could take that away from me now.

I also now considered myself to be a Christian. Not quite a Catholic yet, my Englishness prevented me from denying my Protestantism, but I attended the chapel on a Sunday, and read the Bible I had brought with me every now and then. It was a pocket New Testament and Psalms, and was the only thing not confiscated upon my enlistment.

Christianity itself and the old-fashioned wording of the King James translation was not something that I understood readily, but I understood it better than I did the Hinduism of the Hare Krishnas, or the wilderness of the unknown I had inhabited before I had embarked on my journey into faith. I was a Christian because it felt right, and because the culture of the Legión around me also led me in that direction. What it all actually meant was hidden from me... for now.

This ignorance about what it was I was supposed to believe was not something that bothered me too much. Christianity was a coat I wore because it was the one that seemed to fit. I was happy with the arrangement. I was a soldier in a Christian Army, and I had never been happier.

Only one disappointment came my way during this time. Not long before we were due to be informed where we were to be posted a recruiting officer came to our company from the GOE, the "Grupo de Operaciones Especiales", the "Special Operations Corp", asking for volunteers. The GOE were the elite of the Legión, a small force of approximately five hundred men trained in various specialist skills such as, maritime warfare, arctic and mountain warfare, sabotage and demolitions, parachute and HALO (High Altitude Low Opening) techniques, long-range reconnaissance, sniping, counter-terrorism and survival, as well as escape, resistance and evasion. This was the company the bodybuilder I had floored wanted to join.

We were asked if we wanted to volunteer, and at first I was reluctant until I was surprisingly asked by the black sergeant if I wanted to. Pleased by the offer I said that I did. The sergeant then presented me before the lieutenant. He was assured that I was physically up to the task, and my heart swelled with pride when he was told by the sergeant that I was one of the best recruits in the company.

Suitably impressed, the lieutenant then turned to me. He rattled off a few questions, but his Spanish was fast and I struggled to understand him. He turned to the sergeant and shook his head before turning back to me.

'Just as I thought,' he said, 'your Spanish is good considering that you have only been here a couple of months, but it is too poor for what we require. Our work is specialised and very hard; much, much harder than you have experienced here. We need you to have a better understanding of the language before we could accept you. However, the report from your sergeant is good, so I recommend that you spend a year or two in your company and then volunteer again.'

I was disappointed as I saluted and turned away, but spurred on by the fact that if I performed well at my company and got a better understanding of the language I could possibly make it into training for the Spanish equivalent of the SAS.

*

A few days later the news came through about our postings and I was pleased to find out that I had got my first choice of Fuerteventura. Pedro had chosen the same Tercio and we clapped each other on the back when we discovered we would be going together. We would both soon be members of the "Tercio Don Juan De Austria", the Third Tercio of the Legión.

'Apparently we will go by coach to Cadiz,' Pedro informed me, 'and from there by passenger ferry to Puerto Del Rosario where the barracks is located.'

Flushed with our success we made our way to the bar to celebrate our good fortune.

While there I got talking to a Czechoslovakian in the training company just below ours. After chatting for a while he offered to sell me some dope. I was running low on my stash, so asked him to show me what he had. Outside, and hidden from the military police that frequently patrolled the bar, he showed me a larger than normal slice that he insisted was as good a quality as the stuff I had been buying. It looked and smelled okay, and it weighed twice as much as the gear from the normal channels. He offered it for the same price I was currently paying.

'Where did you get it?' I asked.

'From some friends outside,' he replied. 'Gangsters, they run a drug racket on the Sol,' he added with pride.

I showed the hashish to Pedro later and he whistled through his teeth when I told him how much I had paid for it.

'He's going to have to be careful,' he said. 'If the NCOs discover what he's doing he'll be in big trouble. So will you if you're found to be buying it from him. No amount of "gangsters" on the outside can protect your butt when you're in here.'

I knew that there were clearly defined - if carefully hidden - channels for the selling of dope, and that smoking hash was technically forbidden, and also that it was some of the NCOs who peddled it. Greed is not the wisest distributor of logic, so when I ran out a few days later, I told the Czech that I wanted some more. He told me to meet him behind his hut just before roll call, so at the appointed time, using a back route behind the huts to avoid being seen, I made my way down to his company. Just before rounding the corner to his hut I heard some commotion and paused. The sounds were unmistakable; someone a few feet away was getting a serious beating.

Nervously I poked my head around the corner. There on the ground was the Czech getting kicked and stamped on by four or five men, and they were no ordinary men, all of them were wearing either corporal or sergeants' gold stripes. Without any preamble, and as silently as I could, I made my way back to my own company where I thanked my lucky stars that I had not been found with him in the middle of a transaction. Although I cannot be certain that he was not getting a beating for something else, I decided that the best thing in future was to buy the goods I needed from the semi-legitimate channels offered.

The Czech was a couple of days in the infirmary, and promptly went AWOL a few days after getting sent back to his company.

The following day I was involved in my own violent disturbance, and it all happened because someone stole my best dress shirt.

Initially, one of the things that annoyed me most about my time in the Legión was the pilfering of kit. It was rife, and bizarrely, as far as I was concerned, it was casually accepted as the normal state of affairs. I suppose I should not have been so surprised considering the type of men who made up the bulk of the Legión, but I was young and more self-righteous than I care to remember. I had not yet grasped the fact that if you had lost something that would get you a caning if missed at inspection, or if you had something stolen from you that would once again mean a beating if discovered lost, the best and quickest remedy to the situation was to steal what you needed from someone else. It was a game of sorts, one that had serious consequences if rumbled, but gradually I grew to understand this.

This particular day, I discovered that the shirt I kept for best was missing. I had a few things go missing before, and this time, in order to try and track down the thief, I had written my name under the flap of the right-hand chest pocket.

It was just a few moments to roll call, so I ran around everyone in the company as fast as I could, lifting flaps to see whether they had my shirt or not. I ignored the insults thrown at me in my desire to catch the scum who would steal from his own mates. Eventually I found him. It was a lad I knew reasonably well, having shared the odd joint and beer together. Without hesitating I bundled him into the company building. At first he tried to protest his innocence, but with others looking I lifted the flap of the pocket to show them that this "mate" had been stealing.

Although it was semi-acceptable to steal from your fellow legionarios, it was completely unacceptable to get caught.

Behind me I heard shouts of:

'Ladrón, hijo de puta!', 'Thief, son of a whore!'

I suppose he thought he had done nothing wrong, maybe someone had stolen his and he had found a solution to his problem by lifting mine, but I was in no mood to be rational. Something in me exploded, and I decided to become judge, jury and executioner. I punched him in the face and threw a swift jab to his stomach. I then grabbed hold of him and threw him against the wall. He looked at me with shock in his eyes as I smacked him in the mouth a few more times. As he fell to the ground semi-conscious, I unceremoniously undid the buttons on the shirt and took it off him.

'If you ever steal from me again,' I whispered in his ear, 'I will slit your throat in the middle of the night.'

Someone shouted out that the sergeant was coming, so we bolted.

Later that day, as we sat having a cigarette in the shade after lunch, I heard another story about the "crazy Englishman" flying from mouth to mouth.

Pedro laughed as I passed him my half-smoked cigarette because he was out of them.

'You are a complete "loco", Mark,' he said. 'You are building yourself quite a reputation.' He finished the smoke all the way down to the filter, docking it out on the ground before continuing. 'I think you will end up one of two ways in this army.'

'What's that?' I asked, intrigued.

'Either as a sergeant or in Pelotón for a long, long time.'

I acknowledged the fact that there was wisdom in his words.

I knew that I could be rash and explosive. Tempered by self-control, these traits could be used to make me into a good soldier, and I had already decided that I wanted to make a career of my life here, hoping that one day I might make the three gold stripes. However, such a character as I naturally had, let loose without control could get me into a whole lot of trouble, so I knew that he spoke the truth, but not even I in my wildest dreams had any idea just how prophetic his words of wisdom were going to be.

A month later someone stole my boots. Within twenty minutes I had stolen a pair from someone else. It seems that there was no plumbing the depths of my own hypocrisy.

CHAPTER SIX

Basic Training Again!

El Espíritu De Marcha,
Jamás Un Legionario Dirá Que Esta Cansado Hasta Caer Reventado:
Sera El Cuerpo Más Veloz Y Resistente.
The Spirit of the March,
A Legionario will never say that he is tired until he falls exhausted:
His body will be the fastest and the strongest.

The journey to Fuerteventura was in itself uneventful.

Just as Pedro had indicated, we took a coach to Cadiz where we boarded a ferry that took us to the Canary Islands. We sailed overnight, and I remember little of the journey, but I do recall landing at the dock in Puerto Del Rosario, the capital of the island. The barracks was hard to miss as we walked from the docks the short distance up the hill towards the front gate. It was a huge and imposing whitewashed building with a four-storey frontage that seemed to proudly declare to all who saw it that the Legión was a huge presence on the island, and was not to be messed with.

Pedro told me that when Spain pulled out of the Sahara in 1975, the Third Tercio of the Legión was relocated here. It was now home to over five thousand legionarios, and shortly it was going to be our home too. We were all excited, wondering again what companies we were going to get posted to, what the officers and NCOs were like, what the food and conditions were like, how we were going to cope, etc.

Pedro whispered in my ear as we stood at ease outside the imposing main gate, waiting like pilgrims to be admitted onto the hallowed ground of the barracks within the walls stretching out before us.

'You get some good hashish here and lots of it,' he said. 'It's a major smuggling route to the mainland from Morocco.'

I was pleased to hear that, having securely fallen into the regular smoking of hashish, one of the legionarios' most infamous of pastimes.

'The goats' cheese is brilliant too,' he said.

I looked at him incredulously.

'It's a famous delicacy all over Spain,' he said by way of explanation as he laughed at my English aversion to anything that might have come from a goat. 'Don't knock it until you've tried it.'

The Spanish love their food, and I had learned that something that was considered a delicacy by them was not to be avoided because of my natural British reticence to steer clear of anything that did not look like battered fish or come in a pie. I did try it the first chance I got, and it is simply gorgeous, especially with olives and fresh bread straight out of the oven. It was quite unlike anything I had ever tasted before, and like the "Turrón" I had grown to love last Christmas, it became a favourite of mine, it still is whenever I visit Spain or can get hold of it here in the UK.

Eventually we were presented to the duty officer who issued an order for us to be led away and fed. After eating we were lined up and approached by a captain. We waited apprehensively as he started to speak. Gradually it started to dawn on us that what he was saying was all wrong, apparently we were not going to be posted to a company at all, instead we were informed that we were going to their basic training camp for a few months.

We were gutted, and as we marched back down from the canteen to the main gate, where we were loaded onto trucks that took us a few miles down the road to a small camp not far from the airport, we wondered what sort of sick joke this was that was being played on us. No one spoke as we watched barren, volcanic Canary Island scenery flash past; no one could believe what was happening to us. Getting turned away from the Tercio was like a bad dream, it was as if we had been sat down in front of a five-course meal only to have it taken back to the kitchen before we could eat it.

Our chins were definitely on our chests as we climbed down from the trucks and presented to the comandante of the training barracks. He was a fat guy with red cheeks, who looked like we had disturbed him halfway through his third bottle of wine. As we listened to his waffle our indignation started to rise. Apparently we were going to join a company of local Canarian volunteers halfway through its own training. He did not explain why this was happening to us, but I imagined it was because they needed us to make up the numbers, or because they were not ready for us at the Tercio yet.

Either way it was a complete kick in the nuts for us. Basic training again! We had been through all this before! We had sweat blood and busted a gut to earn the right to wear our Chapiri with pride, in our hearts we classed ourselves as fully fledged legionarios, and now we were being told to relinquish all that and go back to square one. It was almost too much to bear.

Only two facts helped to mildly assuage our growing anger, and those only slightly. The building we were billeted in was brick built and well kitted out, unlike the metal corrugated cowsheds at Ronda, and the thought of a night's sleep not interrupted by the heartless cold of an Andalucían winter under a thin blanket was a pleasing prospect. Still, by the time the officer commanding the company we were being posted to made an appearance we were almost mutinous.

Up until this point my assessment of the officers commanding the Legión had not been a good one. I had never seen them get dirty or muck in at any point of my training. They all seemed to carry a haughty arrogance around with them that perfectly matched the ceremonial white gloves they constantly wore. They were aloof and distant to the point of arrogance, and were disparagingly referred to as "Academia" by the rank and file, an insult that pointed to the fact that they had come from the Spanish Army's version of "Sandhurst"; a place that seemed to breed men with a superiority complex the size of Gibraltar. They disappeared for days on end, only to turn up in packs when there was something ceremonial in which to get involved.

We did not respect them, purely and simply because they were not interested in earning it. They sauntered around like they had invisible broomsticks up their backsides, and expected us to defer to them simply because they had pips on their shoulders. That has never worked in the history of soldiering; ask any soldier from Alexander the Great through to Caesar, Nelson and Churchill. A good leader will win the hearts of his men by getting alongside them and giving them a little respect.

It was not hard to do, we did not expect much after all, we knew we were mere foot soldiers and that someone had to lead. I discovered then that admiring any man who looked at you like you were a bad smell was not even remotely possible. These guys might have been able to inherit their status because their families were rich and because they had been able to afford a good university, but as far as most of us common legionarios were concerned, they were all worse than morons.

Early on in my career I had decided that the men to follow were the sergeants and corporals. They were the men who ate the same dirt, smoked the same dope and spoke the same language as me. They might batter me senseless and run me ragged in their desire to make a soldier of me, but gut instinct told me that they would be by my side if the going got tough. Even though most of them were complete sods, I knew I could trust them - something all men needed to know if those commanding him expected him to face bullets under their charge.

Needless to say, I did not trust the officers, and had never seen any reason to, so when this young good-looking sub-lieutenant called us to attention, I expected more of the same old rubbish. Only this time things seemed to be different. He smiled, spoke to us with genuine affection in his voice, and acted as if he actually cared about our welfare. I was intrigued and even more surprised when my anger started to dissipate in the face of his charm.

Later, after the affable sub-lieutenant had dismissed us, and as we were storing our kit next to the bunks we had been allocated, I asked Pedro what the score was with the officer. Why was he so different?

'Apparently he's a Caballero Legionario,' he replied by way of explanation.

I whistled through my teeth in surprise.

Technically, any man who joins the Legión as a common legionario is entitled to class himself as a "Caballero Legionario" a "Gentleman Legionario". Officers themselves are not allowed to call themselves this; it is reserved purely for the ranks. It was all pants as far as I was concerned, and meant nothing to me, but what did make it special was that if someone progressed through the ranks from legionario to officer, he was still entitled to class himself as such.

I had heard about these men, but I had never met anyone who had done it. I even thought they might have been an urban legend, a myth created by the officers themselves, a legend there to inspire us to do better in the hope of advancement, but something specifically designed to be an achievement beyond our capability. I had no doubt that the officer class guarded their ranks jealously; it is ever so in the world of the privileged. This guy must have been something special to get where he was, especially because he was so young, still in his twenties.

After being dismissed, the rest of the day was our own, possibly because they imagined we had had enough of a let-down being sent back to basic. That night over a beer I took time out to question the other lads in the company we had just joined about the sub-lieutenant.

The amazing thing was that not one of them was prepared to say a bad word about him. They told me that he had joined as a volunteer at seventeen, was called Emilio Torres, a typically verbose and poetic Iberian name, and that he was a local lad, born in the Canaries. They said that he was hard, but fair, caring about them more than was normal for an officer. They then related how he had even gone so far as to get one lad compassionate leave to go to his grandmother's funeral when it had initially been turned down by headquarters.

Apparently he expected you to work hard and did not like slackers, but he bought the whole company a beer the week before last when the pay was late coming through, and he frequently handed out his own cigarettes if no one had any.

He sounded too good to be true, and now I was intrigued beyond measure, but before I decided that I liked him - something I was already finding it hard not to do - I wanted to suss him out myself.

The next morning we were taken for a run, and to my surprise the sub-lieutenant turned out to join us. As he picked up the pace from the front we quickly realised that he was going to see what these new lads he had received into his company from the peninsula were made of. Not that we were slouches; we could manage eight kilometres in less than forty minutes easily. We could march all day if need be, sleep a couple of hours and march all day again, but this morning we realised we were going to be pushed way beyond our normal comfort zone, and at a pace we could barely keep up with.

An hour passed, and the pace had not slackened, it was relentless. The sun was scorching hot, and I could already feel my forehead and nose beginning to burn. Because it was windy, the harsh volcanic dust that made up what the Canary Islanders laughingly called top soil started to clog our mouths and throats, forcing us to spit out thick black phlegm at every few paces. Sweat ran down our faces stinging our eyes, and our T-shirts stuck to us as if we had just walked out of the shower. Our lungs desperately sucked in hot air as fast as we could get hold of it, and as we scanned the horizon for any clue as to when we were nearing the finish I gritted my teeth and prayed that my legs would not decide to stop.

Eventually, after another half an hour, the camp came back into view, and it then became a race to the finish. Naturally the sub-lieutenant was first, he was obviously an outstanding runner, which was probably why he had ordered the run in the first place. I finished twelfth out of sixty and was reasonably pleased with myself, never having been much of a long distance runner. After a drink of water and a smoke, only two-thirds of the company had made it back, and the sergeant loudly declared that anyone not back within fifteen minutes was going to get extra cleaning duties.

I looked around for Pedro; he was not back yet. I was surprised; although not a good runner he was no sluggard. I asked permission to go back and see if it I could find him, only to be told that if I left and did not make it back by the deadline I would cop for the punishment as well. I shrugged, what were a few extra hours cleaning toilets when all I had already got my doctorate in it? Since joining up I had learnt as much about cleaning and scrubbing as I had about fighting. God alone knows how many floors I had mopped and toilets I had cleaned. I was beyond caring, so I set off back the way I had just come.

After half a mile I found Pedro. I had never seen him so beat. He was struggling to get his breath and he looked like he would flake out any minute.

'What's the matter, mate?' I asked.

He stopped and rested his hands on his knees, his face pale and drawn.

'Promise me you will not mention what I tell you to anyone else?' he asked.

'Jura!' I replied; invoking the promise I had already made in Ronda.

'I never told anyone I was slightly asthmatic at the medical,' he replied with a wry grin.

'Hell fire, Pedro!' I laughed. 'How have you managed so far?'

'It's the dust that's done for me this time I think, normally I'm fine,' he replied.

I looked back the way I had come. There was no way I was going to get him back before the deadline.

'Let's walk back,' I said.

'Damn,' Pedro said, spitting a load of dust and phlegm onto the ground, 'I hate to make a bad first impression.'

'Not only have you made a bad first impression, mate, but now we have a load of toilet cleaning coming our way too.'

He shuddered, but who wouldn't if they had seen a toilet block after five hundred drunken legionarios had finished with it on a Friday night.

When we staggered back, the last to make it, I was surprised to see the whole company turned out and stood at ease outside the company building.

'Heads up, Pedro,' I whispered, 'the officer's there.'

'Damn,' Pedro muttered as he lurched into a tired jog in an attempt to assuage any anger already due to come his way.

When we got back we presented ourselves to the sergeant, who promptly launched into a tirade about men not being fit to serve in the Legión who can't stand a hard march.

After the public berating the officer came forwards.

'Why did you go back when you had already finished?' he asked me directly.

'Because he's my friend,' I replied honestly, gesturing towards Pedro, who looked like he was ready to faint.

Instead of another dressing down, which I was expecting, he smiled, reached into his pocket and pulled out a packet of cigarettes.

'Smoke?' he asked.

I took one and accepted the light he offered with it, wondering what sort of strange parallel universe I had just landed in.

He then turned to the rest of the company.

'I want you to recite the Spirit of Comradeship,' he commanded.

This we all duly did.

'El Espíritu De Compañerismo,
Con El Sagrado Juramento De No Abandonar Jamás Un Hombre En El Campo,
Hasta Perecer Todos.'
'The Spirit of Comradeship,
With the sacred oath of never abandoning a man on the field of combat,
Until all perish.'

The company was then dismissed and sent for a shower, and we were both instantaneously absolved of the extra cleaning duties.

As the sub-lieutenant turned away back towards the officers' mess and his lunch, I was left wondering how it was that some men were so comfortable in command, seeming to take to leadership like a duck to water. With some it was a confidence that stemmed from arrogance and ego, and spectacularly failed to secure the respect of those subordinate to them. For others, that special few, of which sub-lieutenant Emilio Torres was undoubtedly one, it came as natural as breathing, and won over completely those who followed them.

No word of explanation was given by him as to why he had acted in such a way just now, there was no need; the Espíritu we had recited clarified more than adequately his meaning. By going back for Pedro I had apparently demonstrated one of the finer virtues of what it was to be a legionario. We have sworn an oath before God to never leave one of our own, vowing to sacrifice all our lives if necessary to bring back a wounded or dead legionario from the field of battle.

Powerful stuff, but I now felt like a complete fraud. I went back for Pedro because he was my friend, and I can honestly say that if it had been anyone else I would not have bothered, but then again this had been a forced run and not a battle. Maybe things would be different under combat, and I tried to believe that under such circumstances I might be able to live up to the sacred oath I had affirmed publicly so many times.

I cannot tell what the officer truly intended, whether it was a calculated way of winning over the new lads to his company, or whether it was because at heart he was a decent man who loved his regiment and the men under his command. Most probably it was a bit of both, but what I do know is that he had categorically succeeded in proving to me that he was a man worth listening to, and maybe even liking. In the space of a few hours, not only had he endeared himself to me and my fellow legionarios, but he had also left me feeling humbled and determined to make sure that I actually did live up to his expectations of me.

Maybe going back to basic here was not going to be so bad after all?

*

A few days later I received a parcel in the post. Inside it was a Good News Bible and a letter from my mum.

There were no restrictions on contact with the outside world, and I had duly informed my family that I had joined the Legión a couple of weeks into basic training. No one was surprised, and generally there appeared to be some relief that I was still alive. Just like she had done when I was in the Merchant Navy, my mum then dutifully started to write me a letter every week.

The letters generally detailed things that had happened in the family, and were often mundane in their content compared to what I was experiencing, but I enjoyed receiving them. They were a reminder of the fact that I did actually have a family, and even if I was currently disenfranchised from it, I also had a place that I came from, a place that had defined me as the individual I was now.

They say that absence makes the heart grow fonder, and although I never missed the strife and conflict of home, I did, like everyone who spends a long time away from their roots, come to miss where I came from. Like most expats it became the concept of England that I missed most, not the reality. Although I did miss the beautiful Yorkshire countryside terribly, the woods, the moors, even the weather came to be things I longed for so much they made my heart ache at times. The truth was that gradually over a period of time I started to miss not home itself, but the idea of home.

When I received my weekly letter, I would find a quiet corner to go and read it. What Mum never said spoke to me more than the words themselves, and for a few tranquil moments I put aside the

Legión uniform and imagined myself standing on the top of Wessenden Head, leaning at a crazy angle in the face of the perpetual gale force wind blowing in from Saddleworth Moor. I sometimes imagined I was walking in the woods on a cold autumn day, watching my frosty breath sparkling in the cold air as leaves dropped like dead gold from the trees, only to be crunched and kicked in great clods underfoot.

At other times in my imagination it would be summer, and I would find myself tickling trout in the river below David Brown's reservoir, before cooking my catch secretly away from prying eyes in foil on a fire in a sheltered dip in the woods. Now and then I would career again like a banshee on my pushbike down my favourite hill. I rode that hill often in my mind's eye. I started just before the road dipped down to the Ford pub and the Isle of Sky road, freewheeling at breakneck speed all the way down to the valley bottom at Meltham Mills. The fun was daring myself not to touch the brakes or stop at blind junctions for the whole mile and a half journey until the bike slowed down of its own accord up the next hill.

Never once did I imagine myself sitting in my bedroom with a razor blade at my wrist, or hating the very air I breathed as I curled up in my own gut-wrenching loneliness. Instead, the letters I received kindled hope, sustaining in me a memory of what had been good about my former life. They filtered the rubbish that had caused me to leave, and left me with a memory I was not troubled in carrying. At those times I dared to believe that one day, in a rosier future, maybe I might be able to go back, but not yet, for now I was a legionario and I had signed away my soul for three years.

My mum had in previous letters told me how she was being "witnessed to" by some Christians at Meltham Mills Parish Church. I had in turn told her about my own decision to become a Christian, and I had received the Good News Bible she sent because I had asked her to send me one. I told her I had lost the other one, but in truth I did not want to explain that it had in fact been used to supply paper for rolling joints when we were short, because the paper was so thin.

This letter was different from her others. In it she was positively gushing with religious fervour, explaining to me in words that almost shone with passion that she was now a "Born-Again Christian". She had been prayed for, and after publicly confessing her sins she had committed her life to Jesus. It all culminated in what sounded like a very real religious experience of salvation, apparent in the fact that she could not stop talking about Jesus. What meant most - and I was unsure as to why - was that she assured me that she was praying very hard for me.

Although I was comforted by the thought of someone praying for me, I truly did not understand what she was going on about when she said that she had been "born again", but she sounded happy and I was pleased for her. I was also pleased because the paper in this Bible was too thick to be used for rolling joints, and it was in modern English. I had struggled with the last one because the writing was so small and because there were way too many "thees and thous" in it. Mainly because it was the only thing in English I could get my hands on, and because I die if I haven't anything to read, I started to read the Good News Bible.

My faith up until starting to read the Bible properly was a complex and strange thing. I was carrying around with me so much religious baggage from all over the place I did not really know who or what I believed. Unfortunately my attitude to Christianity then was a product of the "tradition" of Christianity that clung desperately to a secular Britain I grew up in; a country that was still reeling from the onslaught of a free-thinking secularism that seemed to want to rubbish the idea of God entirely.

I never accepted any of it because it was "establishment", and even though my heart unerringly led me in God's direction, I was as anti-establishment as you could get. If the powers that be wanted me to believe in their idea of God, then out of spite I would not. Besides, it was never put across in a way that excited my thinking.

Yet paradoxically I had never been without the belief that there was a God. Even as a child the reality of God was ever present, and the thought of Him actually existing astounded me. I believed that there might be a creator of everything that had been, and I reasoned logically that if there was a being as large and powerful as to have created time and space, then it stood to reason that the material universe I inhabited could indeed be His creation.

Yet from my time with the Krishnas, I had also inculcated their form of Hinduism into my disjointed faith as well. Their zeal and the complexity of the Hindu philosophy itself - that is so much more than merely worshipping idols – were profoundly influencing my thinking. I was intrigued and drawn to their idea that all things were God, even the trees and stones, and that the highest form of self-realisation is to "know" that you are God in your own right. It somehow made sense to me that I was a part of a larger being. That God abided in me. That I was a spark thrown off the larger fire, and that I carried the attributes and nature of the fire, but none of its grandeur or power.

Their concept of eternity also fascinated me. Described as an endless cycle of reincarnation, the thought of life and death through countless cycles of creation left me in awe of time itself, and I grew fascinated by the impossibility of imagining eternity. Their religion says that many universes have been born and died, and that each one is nothing more than the God Shiva breathing in and out.

One of the instructors at Chaitanya College described eternity to me like this:

'Imagine that the whole earth was made of sand,' he said, 'thousands upon trillions of small grains, right down to the core itself. Now imagine a small bird that would come to earth and take one tenth of one grain every million years. Even when it flies back to take the final tenth of the last grain, you have not even started to begin eternity.'

Naturally, one of my favourite forms of recreational thought while under the influence of hashish was to idly roam in this eternity and the strange world that was my own take on religion. I imagined in my drug-addled mind that I was indeed living in an endless cycle of life and death that had happened so many times before. It absolved me of my apathy, encouraging me to accept what was happening to me as "karma", my fate. It somehow made life easier to bear knowing that it had all happened before, and that sometime in the future, when the endless cycle of life and death was over, I would find the heavenly planet and live in peace.

Yet all this started to get challenged by the words in the Bible I was reading. It said that there was but one life, and that when it was over I would have to account for how I had spent it. It stated that I was a sinner, and declared quite unashamedly that unless I found freedom through Christ, Hell was where I would end up.

This troubled me profoundly and was hard to bear. The concept of personal sin was difficult to understand, and disturbed me. Up until then I had blamed the world around me for my problems, finding some relief in my own sense of self-pity and anger at the way life had treated me. Now I was being told that I had to take responsibility for my own actions and that I had to seek out the forgiveness offered by God that Jesus Christ came to bring to the world.

Naturally I stopped reading.

I put the Bible away in my locker and tried to go back to my own organic way of thinking, deciding that it was easier on the mind and soul, and did not interfere with my life too much if I made up my own faith. I still nodded in the direction of God, respecting the fact that there must be something out there, but I was not yet ready to get to grips with the fact that I was a sinner. I suppose it was that fact that undermined me from that point on. My "sin", once I was confronted with it, became obvious. I was not just a recipient of injustice and pain from other people; I was also a dispenser of it to others.

How I wished then that I had never picked up that damned Bible, because instead of offering me the relief it promised, all I found within its pages was condemnation and guilt. Mentally running away did not seem to help either, because as hard as I tried I could not leave what I had read alone.

The whole "sin" thing grated on me like a stone in the shoe. It plagued me constantly, and my mind did somersaults trying to wriggle out of what I had read. I passionately wanted to believe that I was a Christian, yet I instinctively knew that I could not be a disciple of Christ unless I believed what was written about Him. I found to my displeasure that the basis of my belief that I was a Christian was being challenged.

I was now in an official quandary. I was tempted towards the Hare Krishnas' Hinduism because their philosophy tickled my ears, and also because they had previously told me that Christ was merely a manifestation of the Supreme Being, Krishna, and that He had not died on the cross, but had instead travelled to India while someone else died in His place at Calvary.

It was something I might have been tempted to believe if the Legión had not reinforced to me the fact that Christ's death on the cross was something important, something I needed to be mindful of if I truly was a Christian. I decided that His death and the manner of it could not be swept aside as something inconsequential in the story of Jesus, but quite what it did mean was as yet beyond me.

Even though the Bible was only brought out and read on the very rare occasions I could face up to it, what I had read previously lingered in my memory, and successfully succeeded in turning my relationship with religion on its head. Gone were my easy dope-induced meanderings through the vast vault of eternity, where I could easily justify my life and the manner of it. In their place came something harder, something that wanted me to face up to a doctrine that was as about as comfortable as swallowing a hedgehog.

It seemed that Christianity might want more of me than I was prepared to give it.

The Hymn of the Legión

Nadie en el Tercio sabía
quien era aquel legionario
tan audaz y temerario
que a la Legión se alistó.

Nadie sabía su historia,
más la Legión suponía
que un gran dolor le mordía
como un lobo, el corazón.

Más si alguno quien era le preguntaba
con dolor y rudeza le contestaba:

Soy un hombre a quien la suerte
hirió con zarpa de fiera;
soy un novio de la muerte
que va a unirse en lazo fuerte
con tal leal compañera.

Cuando más rudo era el fuego
y la pelea más fiera
defendiendo su Bandera
el legionario avanzó.

Y sin temer al empuje
del enemigo exaltado,
supo morir como un bravo
y la enseña rescató.

Y al regar con su sangre la tierra ardiente,
murmuró el legionario con voz doliente:

Soy un hombre a quien la suerte
hirió con zarpa de fiera;
soy un novio de la muerte
que va a unirse en lazo fuerte
con tal leal compañera.

Cuando, al fin le recogieron,
entre su pecho encontraron
una carta y un retrato
de una divina mujer.

Y aquella carta decía:
"...si algún día Dios te llama
para mi un puesto reclama
que buscarte pronto iré".

Y en el último beso que le enviaba
su postrer despedida le consagraba.

Por ir a tu lado a verte
mi más leal compañera,
me hice novio de la muerte,
la estreché con lazo fuerte
y su amor fue mi ¡Bandera!

Nobody in the Tercio knew
Who the legionario was,
Who with great recklessness
Enlisted in the Legion.

Nobody knew his history,
But everyone supposed
That he had been bitten painfully
In the heart by a wolf.

And if anyone asked him he would answer
In great pain.
I am a man who has been wounded
By the claws of a wild animal.
I am a bridegroom of death,
And I am strongly bonded to my loyal companion.

When the fight was fierce,
Defending his flag the legionario advanced.
And without fear of an eager enemy,
He knew how to die bravely
In order to rescue the flag.

And as his blood watered the dry land,
The legionario murmured with an aching voice.
I am a bridegroom of death,
And I am strongly bonded to my loyal companion.

When at the end they recovered his body,
Against his chest they found a letter,
And the portrait of a divine woman.

And the letter said,
'When one day the Lord calls you,
I will come for you and claim you',
So with a final kiss
And farewell he was consecrated.

By going to your side,
My loyal companion,
I am now a bridegroom of death,
And I am firmly bonded
To my love and to my flag.

The Song of the Legionario

Soy valiente y leal legionario
soy soldado de brava legión
¡Pesa en mi alma doliente calvario
que en el fuego busca redención!

Mi divisa, no conoce el miedo,
mi destino, tan sólo es sufrir;
mi bandera luchar con denuedo
hasta conseguir vencer o morir.

Legionario, legionario
que te entregas a luchar,
y al azar dejas tu suerte,
pues tu vida es un azar
Legionario, legionario
de bravura sin igual,
si en la guerra hallas la muerte
tendrás siempre por sudario,
legionario
la Bandera Nacional
¡Legionarios a morir!
¡Legionarios a luchar!

Somos héroes incógnitos todos,
nadie aspire a a saber quien soy yo,
¡mil tragedias de diversos modos
el correr de la vida formó!

Cada uno será lo que quiera,
nada importa su vida anterior,
pero juntos, formamos Bandera
que da a La Legión el más alto honor.

Legionario, legionario
que te entregas a luchar
y al azar dejas tu suerte
pués tu vida es un azar.
Legionario, legionario,
de bravura sin igual,

si en la guerra hallas la muerte
tendrás siempre por sudario,
legionario,
la Bandera Nacional
¡Legionarios a luchar!
¡Legionarios a morir!.

I am a loyal and valiant legionario,
I am a soldier of the brave Legión.
It weighs like agony on my soul,
To seek redemption in the fight.

My motto is to know no fear,
My destiny is to suffer alone,
With my flag I will fight with boldness,
Until I conquer or die.

Legionario, legionario,
Who is delivered to the fight,
Leave your fate to chance,
Because your life is a gamble.

Legionario, legionario,
Of unparalleled ferocity,
If you should find death in war,
You will always have as your shroud,
Legionario,
The National Flag.
Legionarios to the fight!
Legionarios to the death!

We are all unknown heroes,
Nobody wants to know who I am,
Thousands of diverse tragedies,
Have formed the course of my life.

Each will be who he wants to be,
Neither is your previous life important,
Because together we form the 'Flag'
And to be the Legión is the highest honour.

Legionario, legionario,

Who is delivered to the fight,
Leave your fate to chance,
Because your life is a gamble.

Legionario, legionario,
Of unparalleled ferocity,
If you should find death in war,
You will always have as your shroud,
Legionario,
The National Flag.
Legionarios to the fight!
Legionarios to the death!

CHAPTER SEVEN

The Third Company of the Seventh Flag

El Espíritu De Combate.
La Legión Pedirá Siempre, Siempre Combatir,
Sin Turno, Sin Contar Los Días, Ni Los Meses, Ni Los Años.
The Spirit of Combat.
The Legión asks that you will always, always fight,
Without turning, without counting the days, the months or the years.

My life as a recruit continued, and I have to admit that rather than hating the time spent going around the training roundabout again, I began to truly enjoy myself. What made it special this time was the comradeship of the training company, which was truly excellent. The Spanish call it "compañerismo", a word that means so much more to me than anything we English have available to use in similar circumstances.

It is hard to describe the feeling and experience of belonging when you are a part of a close knit band of men who come to trust and rely on each other completely. There is a sense of knowing your place, which is both comforting and emboldening. You develop a confidence in those around you that - apart from the proverbial "bad apple" - means you trust one another implicitly. Your own life becomes enmeshed with the men with whom you share your time. For a special and significant part of your life, the whole becomes more important than the parts that make it, and because that whole has a function and a purpose that means something to you, you do not mind handing over your life to it.

I was never prouder, and never happier in uniform than then, and I cannot help feeling convinced that one of the reasons we became such a good unit was because we were well led by the subteniente. It is often said that an army is always a reflection of its general. Good general - good army: poor general - poor army. I know that this might be seen as an oversimplification by some, but I have sailed with good captains and mediocre ones, I have served under good officers and poor ones, likewise I have worked for good bosses and appalling ones, and I have never found this generalisation to be incorrect.

Everything was done because we wanted to be the best, and not because we were forced into something that we were resentful of or truly struggled to attain. We put one hundred per cent into what we did because we believed that the man leading us deserved that, and because we wanted him to be proud of us. When the day of our passing out parade came and went - again - I was genuinely sad to know that I was going to be moving on. I would have gladly spent what was remaining of my three-year contract right there in that training company.

I remember thinking on that day as we recited The Spirit of Suffering and Endurance on the parade ground, our hearts full of pride and joy, just before we were proclaimed "Caballero Legionarios", that I would have followed this particular subteniente into the jaws of hell itself.

'El Espíritu De Sufrimiento Y Dureza,
No Se Quejara De Fatiga, Ni De Dolor, Ni De Hambre,
Ni De Sed, Ni De Sueno; Hará Todos Los Trabajos, Cavara,
Armstrara Cañones, Carros, Estará Destacado, Hará Convoyes,
Trabajara En Lo Que Manden.'
The Spirit of Suffering and Endurance,
Do not complain of fatigue, nor pain or hunger,
Nor thirst or tiredness; do all the jobs necessary, digging,
Dragging cannons or carts, and making convoys,
Do anything you are ordered to do.'

Yet all things come to an end, and it was now time to join the Tercio, and to enter our respective companies. I had previously been asked which company I wanted to join, and felt honoured when the subteniente asked me to consider his company, the Caballería, a lightly armoured cavalry unit. He was to be posted back there when our training company was finally dispersed to their new regiments. I was tempted because I knew that the cavalry only got the best of the new intake, but it was here that I have to admit to making a decision based upon emotion rather than sound reasoning.

I found out that there was another Englishman in the Tercio. He came to see me when he was posted on guard duty at our camp. He was called Paul and had been in the Tercio for over a year. He had also been in the French Foreign Legion, but had to scarper after he had an affair with an officer's wife. He had worked for a while as muscle for a low-level gangster in Liverpool, who had sent him on a job to clear out some squatters in a villa owned by a friend on the Costa Brava. It was there he had heard about the Spanish Legión and decided to give it a go.

We seemed to hit if off when we chatted over a beer. He was a jovial guy who obviously enjoyed a drink and a smoke, but more to the point was that he was dead keen to have a fellow Englishman in the company. The only thing that put me off him slightly was that he was quite disparaging about the Spanish Legión, claiming often that it was not a patch on the French, but I half knew that already, and I found it easy to forgive someone who I could converse with in my own language.

He also told me that there was another lad in the company who spoke English, a Spanish guy called José, who had lived most of his childhood in London, only to be collared for conscription when his family moved back to Spain. He had volunteered for the Legión at intake; apparently this was something conscripts were allowed to do. The upside to such a decision was more money in the pay packet; the downside was a two-year posting rather than the compulsory one year that all Spanish lads had to complete back then.

At this stage I was not really bothered where I went. Paul persuaded me that it would be better to have someone experienced like him to show me the ropes of company life, so, because I also thought that it would be great to serve with my fellow countryman, I agreed to ask for the same company. The subteniente was disappointed, but understood that I wanted to be with a fellow English speaker, so my request to join the third company of the seventh flag was granted.

Pedro had asked for the same company as me, but instead he got posted to the fourth. We were both sad that we would not be together, but at least we would be in sister companies.

*

A few days later we were loaded onto trucks and driven the few miles to the front gate of the barracks. This time we were convinced that there would be no turning us away, this time they were going to let us stay, and we were about as excited as it gets to be finally admitted to the hallowed ranks of the Legión, the elite fighting unit of the Spanish Army.

After being presented to the duty officer at our company hut, I was given a bunk and informed that I was going to be a part of a mortar team. The corporal in charge seemed like a laid-back sort of guy, but Paul sounded a bit jealous when he heard that I was mortars.

'You jammy sod, your lot get to ride everywhere in Land Rovers, while us poor infantry slog it up hill and down dale,' he moaned.

Later that evening, after I had unpacked into my locker, we went for a beer in the bar. While chatting, I tried to dispel the notion that José was not a particularly nice guy.

Foreign volunteers, because they sign up for three years - instead of the two allowed to Spanish volunteers - were paid three times as much, and it became apparent to me after listening to the two of them together that he had been sponging off Paul quite heavily. He was obviously made uneasy by my appearance, wondering how it might affect the dynamics of his relationship with Paul. He probably thought that I was going to upset his meal ticket.

Paul was easy to like. He was tall with an easy smile and a laid-back disposition, the sort who did not bother too much whether he was out of pocket after a night out as long as he had a good time, whereas José was shifty with a furtive demeanour. My first impression was that he was extremely manipulative, unable to maintain any sort of eye contact, and only seeming to be interested in how much money Paul and I had in our pockets, and hence how we, or rather he, could spend it.

He kept going on about the best people to buy dope from, and even talked about us setting up our own little dealing network. I was reminded about the Czechoslovakian who tried that at Ronda, and declined.

Still, José spoke English, which meant that he was company, and Paul assured me that underneath everything he was all right, so I decided to join the gang. There was very little option anyway. The last thing I wanted to do was make enemies on my first day by rejecting their offer of friendship.

They did fill me in on certain aspects of company life, and I was pleased to hear that my new life was not going to be very different from training. This might sound strange to someone who passes from basic to regimental life in the British Army, but there was method in the Legión's madness. The Legión prided itself on the fact that it was supposed to be on a constant war footing. Life in the barracks was, therefore, deliberately hard, frugal and minimalistic. All home comforts were kept to a bare minimum and, true to form, everything was done fast. From when the bugle blew in the morning you were allowed a whole minute to get out of bed, make it, get dressed and formed up, to the time given for morning ablutions – a very generous five minutes to wash and shave.

I had also imagined that the discipline in the company might have been a little bit more casual than training, but that same evening I got an introduction to the fact that it was not.

We were formed up for the last roll call of the day before we bunked down. I had formed up sharp, and, being tall, put myself on the left-hand side facing the duty NCO. Unfortunately, because lance corporals would often jump into the file late, pushing those who were there to the end, I found myself out of line and having to make my way to the far right.

I had had too much to drink, and was feeling rather cocky as a brand new fully fledged legionario, so I sauntered rather than ran to my new position in line. Regrettably for me I did not move fast enough for the sergeant taking the roll call. He called me over and hit me so hard across the face that I hit the deck semi-conscious. When I got to my feet, my head still spinning, I ran rather than sauntered to my new position.

After we had been dismissed, I was tentatively checking inside my mouth to see whether the blood I had just spat out was soon going to be accompanied by a tooth, when Paul came over smiling.

'Welcome to the third company, mate,' he said offering me a toke on a joint behind the hut.

I managed a smile back through the swelling, deciding that I would never let my guard down like that again.

That night, a lad standing guard in the tower behind our hut on the boundary wall shot himself in the head. Paul told me that he was the third suicide that year already.

After breakfast and before that day's orders, Paul had a rant.

'They give you sixty-five bullets when you stand guard here, the idiots,' he said, spitting into the dust. 'Sixty-five sodding bullets to guard what?' he questioned, gesturing around him.

I had to agree; Fuerteventura was not exactly Vietnam.

'It's not as if we are expecting to be attacked. We're not at war, it's a bloody disgrace. Some of these Spanish lads get really homesick.'

I shrugged. Having personally come close to suicide many times, I could understand why someone with a bullet available would choose to end it that way.

'Quick though,' I said.

'You'd think so, wouldn't you?' Paul replied with a wry smile. 'Except that one lad last year managed to shoot his lower jaw off. He now eats everything through a straw. Got sent home though, the lucky sod.'

'You want to go home?' I asked, surprised.

I was as happy as I had ever been in my whole life, and the thought of going home was almost depressing. He merely nodded.

I felt sorry for Paul then. He was from a close knit Irish family and had a wide circle of friends. He had something back home worth missing, and a life he was looking forward to getting back to. I had nothing like that to long for.

*

The first few days changed into weeks, then months, and I settled into Legión life like a duck to water. I enjoyed the mortar training and particularly delighted in the fact that on manoeuvres we got a pistol and sub-machine gun instead of the heavy CETME semi-automatic assault rifle to lug about. My assumptions about the Legión being hopelessly outdated were confirmed during this time. Many Spaniards I spoke to recognised the fact that they were behind the times; some even resented the fact that as a supposed martial nation they could not hope to field an effective armed force in the event of war. However, hope was kindled that things would improve by Spain voting in parliament to join NATO the previous year.

Personally I couldn't have cared less whether the Legión was poorly trained or not; I was still enjoying myself too much to bother about such things. I was a born soldier. By this time I was fit and healthy, and had become in every sense of the word a legionario. My world was the Third Tercio, and everything else disappeared off the map of my consciousness.

One day the captain called me into his office and startled me by saying that my sergeant had recommended me for the lance corporal's course. This was an unusual honour for a foreigner to be recommended so quickly, and I dared imagine that I could aspire to the rank of sergeant in time. Needless to say, by this time I had decided that I wanted to make a career of it.

I was also realising that I had joined the wrong company.

Although I liked Paul a lot, he frustrated me more and more as I got to know him. Mainly because his heart was not in his soldiering, he could be very sloppy and was constantly getting pulled out on some minor misdemeanour or another. He also drank and smoked too much, finding in the bottle and the dope a means to blot out his homesickness. Not that I did not drink to excess, I did often, but because I cared about my soldiering I never let it interfere with my responsibilities.

His constant moaning about how poorly trained and armed the Spanish Legión was compared to the French also grated on me continually. Any excuse was found to ridicule the Legión or to poke fun at it, and I started to realise that my loyalty was being undermined. Gradually I found myself disassociating myself from both him and José, who was finding more and more bizarre means to beg or borrow money from me.

My detachment was taken personally by both Paul and José, and they ramped up the pressure on me to choose either their friendship or my unit. My head wanted to choose my unit, but peer pressure is what usually rules the heart, and I was torn. I knew that if I wanted a career I had to make a choice, and in normal circumstances I would have weathered their displeasure to choose the Legión, but there is always something, or someone, to spoil the party. Mine came in the form of one particular individual. He was an officer, a lieutenant by the name of Olivedo, and all he succeeded in doing was injuring my love for my new home.

He was about as poor an officer as the subteniente on my basic training course had been good. Like most "Academia" officers, he was arrogant and full of his own self-importance. Those flaws I could have ignored, but he also had two other major defects: he was malicious to the point of being sadistic, and he hated everything English.

Before my arrival he had given Paul a particularly hard time, but then again Paul was his own worst enemy, managing by his actions to antagonise Olivedo and succeeding in reinforcing the teniente's conviction that the English were a race of men worth hating and despising. I wondered whether he had been personally harmed or insulted by one of my countrymen, because his hatred was vitriolic at times. Quite why he hated the English so badly did not become evident until a little later on.

I quickly realised that when Olivedo was on duty I had to make sure that everything about me was as faultless as I could make it, and I could see the frustration in his eyes if he could find nothing to berate me about. This way I managed to avoid a lot of punishment, while Paul stumbled from one crisis to another, foolishly giving Olivedo excuses to punish or deride him.

On one occasion, the company had been on what was called twenty-four hour "reten", or "reserve". This meant that for a full day we were on call in case there was any immediate need for troops to be deployed anywhere in the world. During this time we were not supposed to leave the hut except to eat. The rules were that we were expected to be fully clothed, armed and ready for deployment at a moment's notice, but more to the point, we were not allowed to sleep, or drink any alcohol at all. To reinforce all this, snap roll calls were called day and night to check up on us.

On this one particular occasion Paul had managed to smuggle himself a few bottles of wine back into the hut. A snap roll call was called; Paul missed it because he was out of his head and fast asleep on his bunk. Unfortunately for him Olivedo was the officer on duty and he was caught. Paul deserved punishment; I knew that, Paul knew that, hell, the whole company knew that he had broken the rules. Olivedo gave him a choice, a beating or Pelotón. Paul chose the beating and Olivedo set about exacting retribution with a spiteful glee.

By the time he had finished with Paul he was unrecognisable. Both his eyes were completely closed, he had severe bruising to the face, a deep cut to the head, and the following day pus started to come out of his right ear. He also alarmingly declared that he could not hear out of it either. There was nothing any of us could do. Olivedo was an officer and, therefore, untouchable.

This incident above all others angered me. I understood that there needed to be discipline, and I accepted it as a part of the life I had chosen; the Legión would not have been what it was without it. However, just like the lance corporal we had in Ronda, who took his disciplinary duties too far, Olivedo was only succeeding in undermining my enthusiasm and what little respect I had for the officer class.

Paul shrugged it off ruefully, declaring that the beating was better than a thirty-day stint in Pelotón. Still, I decided that if my opportunity came, I would let Olivedo know exactly what I thought of him and his heavy-handed tactics.

My opportunity came a couple of weeks later when I found out why Olivedo hated the English so much.

*

It was a Sunday morning, a day set aside for relaxation, apart from those on guard or other essential duties. After morning parade we were all sitting around underneath the metal canopy at the front of the company hut, a place where we were often instructed in matters of etiquette or Legión history. This time Olivedo was taking it and he veered off into politics. I was disinterested and my mind was wandering until I heard the word "Ingles" uttered a few times.

I looked up and noticed that as he was speaking, Olivedo could not help but look in my direction every few seconds, a sly smile on his face.

I started to listen intently then.

Apparently - and like most right-wing political sympathisers - he had a huge chip on his shoulder about Gibraltar and how it should be returned to Spain. He declared bombastically that the English sat there like vultures on the Rock, in possession of land that should rightly be Spanish and that we had "stolen" it. The fact that ninety-nine per cent of Gibraltarians wanted to remain British subjects, and that Spain was doing exactly the same thing at Ceuta and Melilla on the North African Coast of Morocco (two enclaves the Spanish argue are Spanish and which the Moroccans just as vehemently argue are Moroccan and should be returned to them) as we were on Gibraltar seemed to blithely escape his memory.

'They think they still have an empire,' Olivedo fumed, 'but everyone knows that they are a weak nation, the "sick man of Europe" who continues to live in the past. They posture and pose, but they are like the king who wears no clothes, wrapped up in their own sense of self-importance, but a laughing stock to the rest of the world. Gibraltar ought to be returned to Spain or taken by force if they refuse, then the English can be sent back to Britain with their tails between their legs like dogs that have been beaten with a stick.'

I understood then what he was trying to do.

I do not think it would be arrogant to say that I was reasonably popular and respected in the company by then. I did my job well and had made my mark as someone who could be trusted to get stuck in. I never grumbled or moaned, and would help anyone who asked if it was possible for me to do so. Olivedo obviously wanted to turn the company against me, and he was trying to do it by working on their patriotic sensibilities.

When he had finished his rant, all eyes were on me, and I was about as angry as you could get without showing it.

'What do you think about this, English?' he asked, his mouth barely able to form the word "Ingles" because it was so twisted with hate.

As his question floated in the air waiting for an answer, his face then took on a triumphant look, and rightly so. I could not answer it as I wanted to without upsetting the whole company and displaying the fact that I endorsed my country's actions in keeping a hold of the Rock of Gibraltar against Spain's incessant demands to have it back. Neither could I avoid saying anything, because I would not be able to live with myself if I let him get away with it.

My mind was doing summersaults as I tried to figure a way out of my predicament, and all the while I kept silent the smirk on Olivedo's face grew bigger.

'Come on, Mark,' one of the black NCOs from Sierra Leone who had befriended me said in English, exasperation obvious in his voice at my silence, 'answer him.'

The NCO's encouragement resolved my crisis and I decided to speak out, but I was going to have to be careful.

'I do not like to get involved in politics,' I said, 'and I am unsure as to the legality of Britain remaining in possession of Gibraltar.'

There was an audible groan from everyone present, who were hoping and waiting with a kind of gallows humour to watch me plait my own noose.

'But,' I continued quickly, 'I do know that Spain has attacked the Rock many times, trying to get it back, only to be beaten back on every single occasion.'

I said this because I wanted to upset Olivedo more than anything else in the world, and my subtle message here was that if the Spanish had failed to take it back after trying so many times, then it was Britain's by right of conquest. I remembered my facts from a visit to Gibraltar when I was in the Merchant Navy. There I had visited a museum that listed the many heroic defences British and local forces had conducted against the Spanish, often against hugely superior forces.

There was gasp from everyone present, and Olivedo's face darkened until it looked like a thunder cloud.

'But like I said before,' I added quickly, 'I try to ignore things political.' I could not leave it there though. I had to somehow get the company back on my side, so I played my trump card. 'Besides, I am a legionario, I am not paid to have any political views. My only concern is that for the next three years I have signed a contract as a soldier of fortune to the Spanish Government, and during that time you have my word of honour that I will be loyal to both Spain and to the Legión. The politicians can go and suck eggs.'

To Olivedo's fury and my surprise, this elicited a round of applause from those gathered around me. That night in the bar I did not have to buy a single drink as my fellow legionarios sought to buy me one. Later the Sierra Leonean corporal also made the unprecedented step of inviting me to have a brandy with him in the area usually roped off for the exclusive use of full corporals.

I could not take my guard down yet though, I was going to have to be careful here as well. Although the black corporal was demonstrating a liking for me, he had knocked a Spanish lad's tooth out the week before for turning himself out sloppily for guard duty. He had a reputation for being violently unpredictable and was feared by everyone in the company.

'That was well done, Mark,' he said with a smile. 'Olivedo is a pompous bastard who needed cutting down to size.'

I thanked him as I cautiously sipped my brandy. As he spoke to me in English I realised by his tone and eloquence that he was a well educated individual.

'I only told the truth,' I replied.

'Did you mean it?' he asked.

'Mean what?'

'That you will be loyal to both Spain and the Legión,' he asked.

I nodded.

He laughed, clapped me on the back and ordered another brandy along with a couple of strong, black espresso coffees. When he got them he turned to me.

'You are a liar,' he said quite casually, watching my face for a reaction.

I kept quiet, wondering what heap of trouble was going to come my way now.

'You are English, and everyone knows that the English are very patriotic. I am from an old English colony, and we understand about you. If you are cut you bleed the Union Jack.'

He then pointed to the Union Jack tattoo on my left arm as if that was proof enough. I spluttered that I was patriotic and loved my country, but that I also took my three-year contract to the Legión seriously.

He shrugged as if he had heard it all before.

'I was as naive as you when I first enlisted,' he said, smiling.

His eyes took on a faraway look for a second. I was unsure how to respond, so I kept silent.

'Let me tell you a story,' he said eventually.

He then went on to tell me what most foreigners do not tell each other – why he joined up. He told me how his father had been a colonel in the army back in Africa, and how he had taken part in a coup to oust the incumbent government. I understood then why he was so well educated. A colonel is a senior officer in any man's army and, as such, his children would have had access to good schooling. The coup had failed, and he and his family had to flee for their lives into the jungle. There he had joined a militia at the age of fifteen and fought a guerrilla war for the next five years.

'We styled ourselves as freedom fighters, but as I grew older I realised we were nothing more than bandits,' he mused. 'Only God Almighty Himself knows the death and destruction I saw in those years.'

For a second I saw the demons in his eyes, and realised then why he was so dangerous; he was obviously carrying around a lot of psychological baggage. You can't have been involved in what he had been without it affecting you emotionally.

He then told me how he left Africa looking for a new life in Europe. In Spain he heard about the Spanish Legión and enlisted.

'I was still a soldier at heart, and I hoped that the Legión might offer me a life doing something I was good at,' he said. 'I passed out and came to the third company six years ago. My first guard was at the west gate, do you know it?'

I nodded.

'Well, the sergeant told me to guard that gate, and to not let anyone in. My Spanish was a bit basic then, so he reinforced his command by telling me that no one was to get into the barracks by that gate. "Ni Dios, Ni Nadie", "Not God, Not Anyone," he said. Naturally I took him literally. I had been taking orders all my life, and if someone told me that no one was to pass, then no one would.' He paused to light a cigarette. 'Later that day, the colonel and all his retinue decided to come into the barracks by my gate. I didn't know what to do. Here was the commanding officer of my Tercio, and he was attempting to come in via a gate that the sergeant had told me no one was to come through, not even God Himself.'

'What did you do?' I asked, intrigued.

'Well, I am a God-fearing man, they had given me sixty-five bullets and I had received very definite orders,' he replied, 'so I cocked the gun and ordered the colonel and his mates to halt.' His face grew serious. 'Do you know what the self-righteous bastards did, Mark?'

I shook my head.

'They laughed. They laughed at me... me!' He prodded his chest theatrically. 'I realised then that those pompous white-glove-wearing peacocks, for all their arrogance and their strutting, knew nothing of war. I did though; I had seen more war than all of them put together. I had seen men, women and children killed, and I had lost count of the number of men I had personally shot by the time I was sixteen.'

I was on the edge of my seat by then.

'Did they stop?'

'No, they didn't, they kept coming.'

'So what did you do?'

'I emptied a twenty-round clip into the air over their heads, and when it was empty I loaded another one. I then shouted out that my sergeant had told me that not even God Himself was allowed in through this gate, and unless they turned around and left I would shoot them. They stopped laughing then,' he said, a huge smile on his face. 'In fact they hit the deck, all of them. Flat on their faces they were, shaking in their boots.' He pointed his finger into my chest. 'Yet not one of them even thought to draw his pistol to defend himself, bloody amateurs.'

'Hell fire!' I exclaimed, imagining in my mind's eye the colonel along with another half a dozen senior officers eating dust as this new black recruit stood over them with his loaded gun, threatening to shoot them.

'You have the potential to be a good soldier, Mark, but for the next few months you are going to need someone to watch your back,' he said ruefully. 'Olivedo is a sneaky sod, and you publicly humiliated him today, something he is not going to forgive too easily. He has friends in the company, and I would not trust him further than I can spit. He will probably try to get back at you in some way. If you want, I will keep my ear to the ground for you, I know who he will use if he wants any dirty work doing.'

I understood the enormity of what I was being told then. It was not unusual for men to get beaten up as they slept, or picked on by others because they had strayed out of line and were not pulling their weight.

'Why would you want to help me?' I asked.

'He doesn't like blacks either,' he replied grimly, 'gave me a hard time too until I got my gold stripe.'

He patted his arm theatrically.

I thanked him.

'What happened to you after your incident with the colonel?'

'I got the beating of my life and thirty days Pelotón, curiously though I was sent on the lance corporal's course not long after I came out. The captain told me that the colonel had personally recommended me, which demonstrates a certain amount of lateral thinking I suppose. He said that anyone who can obey an order the way I did was someone he would rather have with him than against him.'

'What's Pelotón like?' I asked, curiously.

He raised his right hand in the air, then made a right to left chopping motion with it as he sucked in air over his teeth. It was the legionario's gesture used when you wanted to demonstrate a hard time, and it was one that needed no words to convey to me the enormity of what he meant.

I shuddered inwardly. If he thought it was hard, then it truly was.

'Now come on, it's your round,' he said.

We both drank too much that night, staggering out just before evening roll call.

The following day it was obvious that my standing amongst nearly all my fellow legionarios had improved, and not just because of my altercation with Olivedo. Most had noticed the black corporal's affirmation the previous evening, and after such a visual gesture of support from a man everyone in the company was wary of, I hoped it would be enough to persuade any of Olivedo's goons from having a go at me. Crazy, violent black corporal on my side or not, one thing was for certain; I was going to have to watch my back. I had upset a nasty man, and he was holding all the aces.

I say my standing was improved amongst "nearly all" my comrades, because Paul and José were disconcerted by the fact that I was increasingly distancing myself from them. Paul because he felt he was losing a mate, and José because he was losing a cash cow. They tried to persuade me that it was foolish to go on the lance corporal's course.

'It's just raising your head above the parapet, mate,' Paul said. 'You become not just responsible for yourself, but for your whole section. Why bring such trouble down on yourself?'

'And you don't get any more money,' José interjected, with typical mercenary callousness.

Maybe I could have weathered all their negative comments without it affecting my zeal, but I saw something later that truly had me wondering whether I had made the right decision to make a career of the Legión.

A corporal in our company, a Moroccan who had been in the Legión for over fifteen years, had a party to celebrate his retirement. He was so excited, full of plans about what he would do when he got out. He told us that he would buy a farm in the foothills of the Atlas Mountains and breed goats. Two weeks later he was back at the front gate, signing on for another three years. I asked the Sierra Leonean why he had come back, especially when he had such great plans.

'Why do you think I'm still here?' he asked me with a shrug.

I replied that I had no idea.

'Because I don't have anywhere else to go,' he said matter-of-factly. 'Neither did the Moroccan. There are lots of us here like that. We have no home on the outside, no family and no friends, and gradually as the years go by we lose the ability to cope with civilian life. Here everything is done for us. We are told when to eat, when to sleep, when to march and when to fight. It's so easy to lose the ability to make those kinds of decisions for yourselves. My guess is that he found life on the outside too scary, so he chose to come back to the Legión, back to the only home he knows.'

I thought about what he said long and hard, and it had a truly sobering effect on me. Did I really want to become so institutionalised that I was not capable of coping with life beyond the Tercio's gates?

Previously the thought of spending my working life as a legionario had enthralled me, now, when I saw the truth of what such a life might bring about, I recoiled from it. The fact of the matter was that I was a little like the Moroccan already. I had no other home, no friends, and although I had a family, I was estranged from them and, besides a miracle, seemingly incapable of being reconciled.

This fear of being institutionalised weighed heavily on me, seriously undermining my resolve to commit to the Legión completely, thereby throwing me in a quandary as to what to do, so I tried to walk on both sides of the fence. Half of me attempted to believe that I could continue as the naive legionario I had originally been, while the other half unwisely hung around with Paul and José, inevitably soaking up their cynicism.

With that and Olivedo's constant malevolent presence in the company forcing me to watch my back all the time, worrying when his retribution would fully manifest itself, over the space of a few months I started to become disenchanted with my new career.

It was not too obvious to those around me. I still enjoyed my soldiering, the physical aspect of it at least, so I worked hard and even got formal confirmation from the captain that I was going to be put forward for the lance corporal's course before the end of the year. Once it enters into you, cynicism is hard to disentangle yourself from. It eats away at your enthusiasm like a cancer, filling you with a listless negativity where there had once been only passion.

I also started to drink and smoke too much, but for that I can make no excuse. I have always had an addictive personality, and I would have gone this way even if I had not started to become disillusioned. One reason was that the beer, wine, cigarettes and hashish were so cheap, and all too readily available. A bottle of rotgut wine cost only twenty pence, and a long six-inch stick of hashish the equivalent of five English pounds. I had nothing else to spend my money on apart from the odd item of kit that needed replacing, or perhaps a meal outside the camp if I felt like it, so I tended to spend most of my money on getting wasted.

On one particular occasion on a Sunday afternoon, while sitting amongst the bunks of our company hut, a young African and I were tripping on a LSD tablet that we had knocked back with copious amounts of wine and dope. He was telling me in a lazy and drug-addled rambling manner about village life back in his home country of The Gambia, but I was not listening. I was not listening because he was slowly turning into a snake before my eyes, and behind him blood slowly started to seep through the walls to drip down onto the floor at our feet.

I imagined that it was some form of witchcraft brought with him from Africa, so I slowly slipped the knife I always had hidden in my boot into my hand ready to kill the huge cobra beginning to raise its head as if to strike me. Only the sudden and half-heard voice of reality in my head reminded me that I was in the middle of a drug-induced hallucination. I fled outside to the fresh air, gulping great lungfuls of it down in an attempt to clear my head. It was too close, and as I shook with nerves, realising grimly how close I came to killing a man in cold blood, I resolved never to touch LSD again; at least until the next time.

I could use boredom as an excuse for my excess, heaven knows that there was not much else to do in our spare time. I could even argue the fact that drink and dope were as cultural to the Legión as fish and chips were to an Englishman, but nothing can really justify the fact that I was completely unable to say no. I have always suffered with a low self-control threshold, and I never did know when to stop when it came to things that were better enjoyed in moderation, or not at all.

Once again, because I had started to lose my motivation, and because I was getting back into serious alcohol and drug abuse, the grim spectre of self-destruction, that malign spirit that had followed me all my life, made an unwelcome reappearance. I once again felt the grip of its bony hand on my shoulder ushering me along the road to perdition. It was a journey I had taken many times before, and it was always a prelude to the complete destruction of whatever it was I was involved in, yet I did nothing to stop myself.

The strange thing was that deep in my heart I longed to be content, to find the place where I could belong - my home. Yet all I seemed to be able to achieve was misery. I was a man at war with himself and, God help me, I couldn't choose a side. It was as if a part of me believed that I did not deserve to be happy, and sought to deliberately rupture anything decent that came my way.

Even now as I write this I am at a loss as to fully understand this masochistic tendency I had then. This subconscious desire I had to utterly destroy myself was like a dangerous alter ego, the mad and violent Mr Hyde to my peace-seeking Dr Jekyll. It truly maddened me. I longed to be free of Mr Hyde on the one hand, yet on the other I embraced him like a lover. It was as if I was in the grip of the devil himself, puppet dancing to whatever tune he chose to play. The bitter truth was that I was unable to choose the freedom I longed for because a part of me was wedded to the jailor's chains.

Yet this time there was one thing different. This time my conscience and my desire to consider myself to be a Christian whispered quietly in the background of my mind, sucking some of the pleasure out of my excess.

'Where is God in all this?' I asked myself in the few quiet moments I had, usually on guard in the quiet of the sentry box in the small hours of the morning, or lying in my bunk after lights out. 'Where is the reason for living in the life I am living, what is my purpose here?'

I had no easy answers. Only the remembrance of the words I had read in the Bible. "The wages of sin is death", it had declared, so I argued back that I was a legionario, a bridegroom of death, I was supposed to have no fear of the grave. I was supposed to walk fearlessly into the shadow of the valley of death arm in arm with the skeleton I was pledged to, confident that the life I had chosen had given me a cast iron guarantee that I was doing okay. I was a Christian soldier in a Christian army, and my reward would undoubtedly be Heaven - or so they said.

As naive and as pliable as I was, even I did not really believe that. There was more to Christ and the cross, I knew there was. Every instinct in me told me that there was a mystery there waiting to be unravelled. I was simply reluctant to admit to it or to pursue it. I attempted to deceive myself, arguing that I was not interested in this God I had glimpsed in the pages of the Bible; instead, I wanted the god of the Legión, I wanted the drink and drugs, and the promiscuity available here. I also wanted the absolution so freely offered by a priesthood completely sold on the lies they propagated themselves. The Christianity of my Good News Bible was too hard an objective for me, and now I wanted to be left alone.

Yet my conscience would not leave me alone. It was like walking with a stone in my shoe, and in spite of my own misgivings sometimes it would inspire me to make an effort to shake off the wild man within me, to get back to the place I had been at when I joined up. Sadly that naive young man had gone. Even so I hung on grimly to my new life, desperately wanting to believe that I had found my reason for living here in the Legión, that this was now my home. Yet I knew in my heart of hearts that it was all starting to fall apart again, and sooner or later it would all blow up in my face just like it always did.

I was back at the top of the helter-skelter, and the only way anywhere was down.

*

Unfortunately for me my premonition was right. I was going to mess up again, but even I did not imagine how fierce or violent the consequences were going to be. This time I was going to a place that would come close to being the death of me.

CHAPTER EIGHT

AWOL – Absent Without Leave

El Espíritu De Acudir Al Fuego.
La Legión, Desde El Hombre Solo, Hasta La Legión Entera,
Acudirá Siempre Donde Oiga Fuego,
De Día, De Noche, Siempre, Siempre, Aunque No Tenga Orden Para
Ello.
The Spirit of Assisting Under Fire,
The Legión, from the first man to the entire Legión,
Will always go to assist when he hears firing nearby,
By day, by night, he will always, always go, even though he has not
been ordered.

My resolution to go AWOL happened quickly, but the circumstances leading up to the decision took a couple of weeks to come to fruition.

Paul came to me heartbroken after apparently receiving some bad news from home. It appeared that his mother had been visiting relatives in Belfast when she had been caught up in a blast from a car bomb, and seriously injured. He had applied for compassionate leave, but it was rejected. He was distraught, and I felt powerless to help him.

'We've got to get him home somehow,' José said to me, 'he'll do something stupid otherwise.'

Naturally I wanted to help my friend, and the captain's decision not to allow him to go to see his badly injured mother angered me. Although at heart I understood the decision; I knew for certain that he would not come back if he got the chance to get back to England, which was almost definitely why he was denied the leave. Still, it was another reason for me to get disenchanted with the Legión.

Although becoming increasingly cynical, I was still clinging to the life I had chosen, and up until this moment I would not have entertained desertion. However, Paul said something that grabbed my interest. He told me how some lads from the British Army's Parachute Regiment had gone AWOL for some misdemeanour and joined the French Foreign Legion during his time there. After some time they left and were welcomed back into the paras after a spell in military prison. The army reasoned that their experience in the French Legion could only benefit the regiment.

'If you love your country as much as you say you do, why don't you join the British Army?' he said, 'It would be better than staying with this shower. Help me get home and join up. You're fit, you already know how to soldier and you love the life, they'll snap you up.'

Paul was not a Nationalist as I was; his family had their roots in Northern Irish Catholicism, so naturally his patriotic leanings did not swing in the same direction as mine, but the idea he planted took root in my mind.

I had originally joined the Legión because I was out of money and luck, and also because the idea of an adventure appealed to me. Now that I knew for certain that I would make a good soldier it made sense to join the British Army. I would be better trained and paid, and there also might be the chance of some action, something I was unlikely to get with the Spanish Army.

A week after the news about Paul's mother being hurt, both Paul and José got me on my own one Saturday afternoon. They had come up with a plan to get off the island. Needless to say it was José's idea, and revolved around them capitalising on my merchant navy experience.

'We could steal a yacht from Corralejo,' he said enthusiastically, 'and sail it to one of the other islands. From there, Paul can get some money sent through from his family while we hunker down somewhere in a cheap dosshouse for a few days. When the heat has died down we apply for temporary passports from the British Consul by claiming to be tourists who have had their passports and luggage nicked, we then make our way home.'

I thought about it. In principle it was a decent plan. Corralejo was the main tourist centre on Fuerteventura, plus it had a marina in which there was a fine selection of yachts. As long as there was an engine, a compass and a few charts I could sail it.

Desertion was no new thing for the Legión, many men had tried to escape, and some had even succeeded. Most had merely not bothered returning after a home leave, but as far as we knew, and far more importantly for my consideration, no one had ever made it off the island without a legitimate permit. The most audacious attempt had apparently been by some Germans a few years back who had tried to hijack a plane having stolen weapons and ammunition from the company armoury. They had failed after deciding not to get involved in a gun battle with the entire Tercio.

Getting off the island was hard because Fuerteventura then was by no means the thriving tourist island it is today. It was still relatively unspoilt. There was only one airport and only two ferries. The airport was five miles from the barracks, there were two or three planes a day and it was easily watched. The ferry at Puerto Del Rosario was a minute from the barracks and dealt with sailings to and from the peninsula; the other was at Corralejo, where we planned to nick the yacht. This ferry ran to and from Fuerteventura and Lanzarote. All three routes off the island were not busy and were monitored assiduously by the military police.

Anyone caught going AWOL, or even being late back to the barracks for roll call, was often sent to Pelotón. Our company hut was only a few yards from the small rectangular fort in the middle of the barracks that was home to the work section. Its whitewashed walls were five metres high and the only way in was by a huge metal door. The brigada who ran it was a huge barrel-chested bear of a man in his late forties whose forearms were covered in home-made tattoos, the sign of a long-serving legionario.

He had a cruel face and spoke with a kind of growl, often associated with someone who had rotted his larynx with wine, cigarettes and hashish. He had a fearsome reputation as a vicious disciplinarian, and was rumoured to have put more than a few of his charges in hospital. The sergeants and corporals permanently stationed there were no better; a more bloodthirsty crew you would never hope to meet. I certainly did not fancy spending any time in their care.

After some thought I refused to help them, not only because I did not wish to spend any time in Pelotón, but also because I could not find it in my heart to dishonour the regiment like that. I had signed a three-year contract and I wanted, for the first time in my life, to see something through to an honourable conclusion. I had by then decided that I would complete my contract and join the British Army when I got back home. I wanted to be a career soldier.

This refusal angered Paul and José, so they decided to give me the silent treatment, ignoring me for days on end and making it known that by turning them down I had lost their friendship. I withstood the silence for over a week, hoping they would come around, but then, to make matters worse, Olivedo found a chance to have a go at me.

*

We were undergoing abseiling training on a forty-foot wall near the assault course. Assembled at the bottom we were given a demonstration by one of the sergeants. After the display, Olivedo, whom I had since learnt had Special Operations aspirations, decided to show us how it was done. Unfortunately for him he rigged himself up wrongly, and as he stepped back off the edge of the wall he fell down onto his backside with a loud smack. It must have hurt like hell. To cap off the comedy of errors he then misjudged where the ground was on the way down and once again fell onto his rear end before he had a chance to put his feet down. It would have been hilarious if it had not been so tragic.

The first person he looked at as he got to his feet was me. I could see the challenge in his eyes, daring me to smirk or laugh. Thankfully I was becoming proficient at developing what soldiers call the "stone face". It is a means by which you keep completely hidden from ranks superior to yours anything you might be thinking. Inwardly you could be swearing fit to bust and full of anger, or laughing yourself silly, but what mattered was that your face remained implacable in its rigid austerity. It is hard graft to perfect, because your eyes are the most difficult part of you to keep hidden, but for me at that moment it was a useful tool. I could not afford to give Olivedo another reason to dislike me.

Pretty soon I was up for my go. The technique we were taught involved wrapping the rope around your body in a certain way and launching yourself over the edge. There were no clips or harnesses, just the rope and you. With my heart beating rapidly I stepped out. Halfway down I got the gist of it and started to push myself away from the wall as I released the rope. I made it to the floor in three jumps and was justifiably pleased with myself.

Olivedo was furious, barely able to conceal his anger at my success. It was then that I realised that no matter what I did, this man was going to hate me. He obviously had a serious psychosis, one that bizarrely manifested itself at Englishmen.

That same afternoon, supervising the assault course he got his chance to get his own back. It was a hard circuit, about four hundred yards around with various obstacles to get over or under on the way. I generally managed it well, but the one part of the course I found especially difficult was the ground net. It was a large cargo net pegged to the ground that we had to crawl under. It was supposed to help us stay flat and move at speed if under fire, but because of the problems with my dislocated hip when I was younger I always found ground crawling, or the "reptile" as the Legión called it, very difficult, taking longer than most to cover the same distance.

Olivedo saw my weakness and publicly berated me, ordering me to go faster, sending me back to complete the same section time and time again. It was humiliating, but I refused to give him the satisfaction of seeing me concede or show tiredness. I kept my stone face even when the repetitious crawling had skinned my knees and elbows so badly they were bleeding. It was not just my elbows and knees though, my back felt like it was being battered by the metal joints in the thick rope as I crawled the twenty metres underneath it time and time again. As the humiliation carried on, I wondered whether I could kill him and get away with it. Officers on duty often slept in the barracks. I could slip past the company guard and slit his throat in the middle of the night. He had so many enemies it would be impossible to prove who had done it, and it was that murderous thought that kept me going.

By the time we were dismissed I was so tired I was barely keeping it together, my legs felt like jelly and my body ached like I had gone twelve rounds with Mohammed Ali. Back at the company hut I drank some water and threw up in the toilet. Later, when showering, I was asked a number of times who had beaten me, only later did I see the bruising on my back - I was black and blue as if I had been flogged.

That evening, after applying a liberal amount of antiseptic to my knees and elbows, I went to the bar and started to get hammered. Paul and José, who had seen what had happened came and again offered me the chance to join them in their desertion plan. It was perfect timing, as full of anger as I was at Olivedo's treatment I agreed to go with them.

In giving my word to join them, I set in motion one of the most dangerous and craziest things I have ever done in my life, and because of it a series of events unfolded that led me to the singular most influential moment in my life. I was going on another adventure, one where eventually I was going to find something so precious my life would never be the same again. First though, I was going to have to learn what it was to suffer more than I had ever imagined possible. Mentally, physically and spiritually, I was going to hell and back.

That evening we recited the Spirit of Union and Help, and I remembered thinking that in a way I was fulfilling the code of it. I was going to the aid of a mate who needed my assistance. I was pretty certain, however, that the authorities would not see what I was planning as a fulfilment of that particular motto.

'El Espíritu De Unión Y Socorro,
A La Voz 'A Mi La Legión', Sea A Donde Sea,
Acudirán Todos Y, Con Razón O Sin Ella, Defenderán Al Legionario Que Pida Auxilio.'
*'The Spirit of Union and Help,
To the cry of 'to me the Legión', wherever it may be,
Everyone will attend to defend the legionario who has asked for assistance.'*
*

It was a balmy Sunday afternoon a few days after my run-in with Olivedo on the assault course; José, Paul and I were discussing our plan over a good few bottles of wine and a couple of large joints. By this time I was regretting agreeing to go, and was hoping that eventually we would talk ourselves out of it. I was crucial to the whole plan because of my seamanship knowledge, so I reasoned that if I could procrastinate long enough the plan might fall apart.

'If we don't go soon we'll never go,' José said, trying to spur us into action.

'But we've got no money,' I replied, 'we'll at least have to wait until next payday.'

'I thought you wanted to help your mate,' he said angrily.

I hated it when he used such emotional manipulation, and wondered how he could feel no sense of guilt at the way he tried to control people. I also pondered inwardly why he was so anxious to leave. It can't have been only concern for Paul's situation; he was far too conniving for that. There had to be another reason.

'I can't wait another two weeks,' Paul said mournfully, 'I've got to get home.'

I felt like I was being boxed into a corner, but at the same time I did wonder how I would cope if I knew that my mother was possibly at death's door and I was not allowed to go to see her. It must have been emotionally very difficult for him, and I felt my resistance lowering.

'We can find some money on the way,' José said, sensing that he might have us agreeing with him. 'I know a bar on the beach just outside Corralejo; it's nothing more than a hut and would be easy to break into. We can probably find some money there.'

This was starting to get serious; as well as stealing a yacht we were now going to be robbing bars.

'Can we be sure that there is a suitable boat at Corralejo and, more importantly, are we sure that there is one there that would be easy to steal?' I asked. 'We at least ought to reconnoitre the place.'

'There's no such thing as a perfect plan,' José replied vehemently, 'but if we do nothing now we never will.'

I thought again about the way Olivedo had humiliated me on the assault course, realising with a sinking feeling that no matter how well I soldiered things were not going to get any easier for me here. That lunatic wanted blood, and now the madman had got his teeth into me he would be hard to shake off, so probably because I did not fancy being Olivedo's whipping post for the next few years, and also because the dope had chilled me out, I reluctantly decided to throw in the towel.

'Okay,' I said, 'let's go!'

'When?' Paul asked, brightening up.

'Why not now?' José said.

So the worst desertion plan ever conceived in the history of the Legión was thrown together. We would get a day pass then make our way to the edge of Puerto Del Rosario where we would wait for nightfall. Under cover of darkness we would walk along the coast north to Corralejo, a distance of just over twenty miles by road, and probably nearer twenty-five hugging the coast by foot as we planned to do. Once at the port, we would find a hiding place and once again wait for night-time, whereupon we would make our way to the marina and steal the yacht. The nearest island was Lanzarote, visible to the naked eye as long as the weather was good. Once there we would have to think up something else until Paul could get money transferred to him.

It was complete and utter madness. We had no money, we would be wearing our dress kit, woefully inadequate for such a march, especially the lace up shoes that came with it, plus we had no food or water to take with us as provisions. Nevertheless, we got our passes and made our way as casually as possible to the edge of Puerto Del Rosario, keeping a watchful eye for any military police who might be patrolling.

The town ended suddenly with a large expanse of open ground about five hundred yards long that looked like it was used as a refuse tip. After that the shoreline took over. It was flat and openly visible for many miles north. Logically we could neither stay inside the town and visible until sundown because the police would probably find us, nor could we set off along the beach because that was too open.

'There,' Paul said, pointing, 'an old bunker.'

Sure enough, halfway between the town and the sea was an old concrete machine gun post, probably dating from the Spanish Civil War. We still had to get to it before sundown, or risk getting caught. There was nothing else to do but to run for it and pray that no one saw us, so with our hearts thumping in our chests we dashed across the ground and made our way inside the bunker.

Once inside we nearly gagged at the stench. It was being used as a public toilet and drug den; there were piles of excreta and needles everywhere. Because of this mess there was nowhere to sit down; neither was there anywhere else to go for another few hours until full darkness descended. The only thing we could do was to squat down on our haunches, try to ignore the smell and wait.

As the sky darkened we kept a nervous eye on our watches. As the time slipped towards ten o'clock the drink and dope started to wear off, and we realised that within a few minutes the roll call would be taken and we would be officially classed as AWOL. There was still time to race back to the barracks and get nothing more than a slap and perhaps a company punishment, or at worst fifteen days Pelotón. None of us mentioned going back though. The die had been cast and we had chosen our route.

Ten came and went, so did eleven. We maintained a tense silence as the enormity of what we had done started to sink in. We were now officially fugitives from the Legión; an army that dealt severely with minor infractions, never mind what we were doing. If we were caught they would do more than throw the book at us, they would beat us to within an inch of our lives with it.

After sharing a tense cigarette we poked our heads out of the bunker and took a look around. There was very little light pollution from the town to highlight our position, and mercifully the moon was hidden behind thick cloud. This was a good sign. If the moon stayed hidden the whole night, once we got out into the country it would be pitch black, offering us good cover.

'Ready?' Paul asked, having assumed control of the operation.

With a nod of our heads we sped across the rest of the open ground down to the shoreline. We now had six or seven hours to try to cover twenty-five miles over unfamiliar ground in the dark. Only after we had gone a few miles did we realise that we were not going to make it. It was going to take at least a couple of nights to get to Corralejo, and we began to regret our haste in not planning to take anything as basic as food and water.

It is an easy thing to do to follow a shoreline when it is nothing more than flat beach, but Fuerteventura was a volcanic island, so as well as sandy beaches we also had sharp flesh-shredding rock to contend with. This slowed us down considerably, as did when the beach disappeared and we had no option but to get up to higher ground next to the road. Unfortunately this meant that we were in full view of any traffic that came along it. We kept up a good pace and maintained single file all the way. As soon as any of us saw a car's headlights we would shout out a word of warning and quickly find cover.

On more than one occasion the unmistakeable sound of Legión Land Rovers would trundle past. Our hearts were in our mouths until we heard them retreating into the distance, hoping to everything we held sacred that we would not hear the sudden screech of brakes and the thud of boots on tarmac signifying that we had been seen. Sometimes the Land Rovers would be little more than a few feet from our heads as we found as much cover as we could behind a bush or rock at the side of the road.

Only later did we find out that the colonel was so infuriated with our disappearance that he told the military police to shoot to kill if they felt that we were either going to resist arrest or flee. He had taken our absconding as a personal insult, and decreed that we would pay severely if caught.

It is strange how the mind can relax even under stress, especially when you are engaged in a physical activity, and on a few occasions as I slipped into the routine of the march, my mind wandered. For a few valuable minutes it was as if it was escaping the tension that was compressing me, like a drowning man coming back to the surface to grab a fresh lungful of air. I even took a few precious seconds to gaze in wonder at the stars when the clouds cleared. The stars have always held a particular fascination for me, especially like that night when they were in full view without the restraints of light pollution diminishing their true glory. There were so many of them, billions, and all of them so far away as to boggle the mind.

However, such temporary respite only made coming back to reality even more difficult to come to terms with. As I put one foot in front of the other that night, how I wished that I had ignored Olivedo's hatred and Paul and José's manipulation in order to persevere with my career. Once again I was walking a tightrope that succeeded in bringing nothing but anxiety to my soul.

'There has to be a place of peace somewhere,' I whispered desperately into the darkness. 'There has to be somewhere where I lay myself down to sleep, secure and free from all this stress.'

Eventually the horizon started to lighten and we decided that we had to find somewhere safe to hole up for the night. After a short while we found a small cave underneath an overhang not far from the sea. There we tried to get some sleep as the sun rose. It was an incredibly uncomfortable place to lie down in, being formed as it was from sharp volcanic rock. Our attempts at rest were severely interrupted by not just the traffic above our heads, but also the sound of the ocean and some loud German tourists on a beach just around the corner from us. Mercifully, in the midst of our shredded nerves and the noise we managed to grab a couple of hours of kip.

That night we waited once again for the sun to set and darkness to descend before picking up the trail north. Our journey was as uneventful as the previous night, but by this time we were hungry and very thirsty, which succeeded only in making the march more uncomfortable. After a few hours dodging vehicles and hugging the coast, the beaches started to give way to what appeared to be a desert complete with sand dunes.

'I know this place,' José said enthusiastically, 'it's a mini-desert they drive sand buggies around on. It stretches for miles. There's also a hotel near here popular with Scandinavian tourists, and it's only a few kilometres from Corralejo. The beach hut bar I was telling you about is just beyond the hotel.'

Sure enough, after a short while we came to a huge hotel. It was an incongruous sight, rising up out of the sand as it did like a giant concrete leviathan. We welcomed its sight though, longing as we were for the chance to find some water and something to eat.

We settled down out of sight in a dip in one of the dunes while Paul went off on his own looking for some clothes and food for us all. We would be less likely to get caught if we had some civilian clothes, being more able to blend in with the foreign tourists that abounded this part of the island. Something else we had failed to think about in our drug and alcohol fuelled desertion plan.

He came back after an hour with only a pair of shorts and a T-shirt he had found beside the swimming pool. He had had to be careful because there was a guard patrolling the hotel, otherwise he would have had a look inside. We decided it would be best if he wore them because he was the one doing all the scouting. José then took us off looking for the beach bar he had mentioned previously.

Eventually we caught sight of it. Like the hotel, the small wooden shack looked a little out of place in the middle of a huge expanse of sand, but it was a welcome sight for us. After checking to see if there was anyone around we made short work of kicking the door in. Inside we found no money or food, but we did find a few litres of bottled water, and brandy.

Outside the sun was making another unwelcome appearance, so we dashed inland farther into the dunes. There we slept, a little more comfortably than the previous day because of the soft sand, but also because the brandy on an empty stomach was a good tranquilliser. The only thing here to spoil our dreams was the loud roar of the odd beach buggy tearing around the mini-desert that made this part of the island so popular with tourists.

Once again, as the sun sank below the horizon and night folded in, Paul went off on his travels. He was gone a long time; so long that both José and I thought that he might have been rumbled by the police. Eventually though, a few hours before daybreak we heard his voice calling us in the distance. He had momentarily lost his bearings and could not remember where he had left us.

'I've found a way into the marina,' he said excitedly. 'There was a police patrol, which is why I was late. They parked up a few yards from where I was hiding. Sat there for hours the sods did; smoking and watching. They have only just left, so if we're quick we can get to the marina, sort out a boat and have it away before daybreak.'

It was the best news we had heard for a few days.

Paul took us by a back route through the town, coming in from the west rather than the south to avoid suspicion. Nevertheless, we felt completely exposed as we made our way through the sleeping town, knowing that we stuck out like sore thumbs, me and José in our by now ragged and torn uniforms and Paul in his shorts and T-shirt. Anyone who looked out of their window would have had no doubt in their mind that we were up to no good.

After what seemed like an age we found our way to the marina. All that stood between us and our prey was a large open area, host during the day to various al fresco bars and a car park. Hiding down an alley we checked to see if the police were around.

'Damn,' I muttered, pointing to a Land Rover with the hated white P M (Policía Militar) stencilled on its side in bold letters parked to one side of the square almost out of view.

The patrol Paul had seen earlier had come back.

Inside we could see the glimmer of a couple of cigarette ends. The sky was lightening and there was no way that we could have made it back to the dunes without being seen. Neither had we passed anywhere that might have proved to have been a decent hiding place on the journey in. We were going to have to wait them out and hope that they cleared off before it was too late.

Our hearts were in our mouths as we waited in the shadows of the alley, every minute seemed like an eternity, but eventually the Land Rover roared to life and took off south towards Puerto Del Rosario. It was now almost light and the unmistakeable sights and sounds of a town waking up started to assault our ears.

There was no other option for it now. We had to get to the marina and find a boat. All subterfuge in daylight would have been pointless considering our physical appearance and the fact that it was probably well known that there were three Legión deserters on the run. We knew that we had to act as relaxed as possible if we wanted to make it across the square without giving the game away, so we walked as casually as we dared towards the marina, eyes front and shoulders square, hoping to God that our bravado and efforts at nonchalance would hide us from suspicion.

Amazingly we made it across without being challenged. José made a dash towards a large motorboat.

'Too big,' I hissed. 'We need something easy to handle, preferably with a sail and a small outboard motor we can start easily.'

'There,' Paul said, pointing towards the end of the wooden jetty we were on.

It was perfect; a small two-man yacht with a five horsepower outboard motor. I climbed on board to check it out as the other two kept watch. There was a small padlock on the door into the cabin that was easy to wrench off. Inside there were two bunks and not much else. I took the tarpaulin off the motor and checked to see whether it had any fuel. We were in luck, it was full. There was also a full set of sails if we ran out of juice. I gave the cord a quick pull to see whether the motor was in working order and was satisfied to hear the grunt of an engine just waiting to kick into gear.

This was where I took over.

'Get on board and down into the cabin, stay out of sight,' I told the other two. 'I will cast off, start the engine and get us out of the harbour. It will look less suspicious if only one of us is visible.'

Paul and José did not wait to be told twice.

Acting as unhurriedly as I could, considering the circumstances, I undid the bow and stern ropes, and started the engine. The beauty started first time, and for the first time in a couple of days I wondered whether our hair brained scheme might just work.

All did not go quite as well as I had hoped though. Merely twenty yards from the breakwater and freedom the engine started to splutter and cough. After a few seconds the power died and the motor cut out completely. I swore very loudly and frantically pulled the cord a few times, only to be greeted with at first a roar then a splutter and finally, silence.

A man setting up fishing gear on the breakwater I had not noticed before looked up as he saw me struggling and shouted out if everything was okay. I smiled and gave him the thumbs up; glad I had asked José and Paul to stay hidden.

Frantically I checked everything as Paul and José's faces grimaced at me from the door of the cabin.

'Stay out of sight,' I whispered, 'there's a fuel problem I think.'

I quickly found what was wrong; the fuel pipe was twisted, restricting the supply of gas to the engine. I straightened it out, paused for a few seconds to allow the fuel to flow before gently tugging the cord a few times to prime the pump. I held my breath and with one last heave we were back in action, and the sound of the engine kicking into life was like music to my ears. I took hold of the tiller, noticing dryly that my hands were shaking. Pretty soon we were past the breakwater and leaving Corralejo behind us. By this time the sun had burst clear of the horizon flooding daylight everywhere, so I pointed us towards the towering sight of a flat-topped mountain on Lanzarote in full view to the north.

When you interrogate your memory of a long time ago, attempting to put together pieces that you wish to recall, some memories come easier than others. Some recollections of years gone by are as if they happened yesterday. For some reason this particular memory has imprinted itself on my mind in such a way that I know I will never forget that exact moment. The journey across the six miles of water from Fuerteventura to Lanzarote was a glorious time for me. I can still smell the salt and feel the soft seawater spray. The sun warm on my back, unfreezing my aching and tired muscles, and nothing but the gentle roll of the sea for company.

The sea was a dark forbidding blue, with only a few white horses rearing occasionally on the crest of a wave nearby. I wondered idly what the currents would be like here as the ocean forced its passage between the two islands, nothing I had seen yet had alerted me to any danger. Thankfully the currents were gentle that day. Above there was nothing but a few high wispy clouds to steal the glory from what was an otherwise clear sky.

It was a beautiful time in an era of chaos, and I will never forget it until the day I die.

Paul and José stayed inside the cabin for the whole journey, struggling with seasickness, and attempting to catch up on some sleep. This was fine by me. I was enjoying the freedom of the ocean, revelling in the dip and weave of the yacht as the small motor powered us steadily towards the huge flat-topped mountain on Lanzarote from which I was taking my bearings. God alone knew what awaited us on the next island, but for now, for a few precious hours, my heart knew a little peace.

In an effort to save fuel, halfway across I cut the motor and hoisted the sail to see if there was enough wind to take us the rest of the way. Only the odd flutter of a weak breeze slapped feebly against the canvas, hardly enough to disturb the sail from rest, never mind power us along, so I started the motor again and hoped that we were going to have enough fuel to make it all the way, because merely drifting in these windless conditions could be fatal.

It must have taken hours to cross the stretch of water between the two islands, but for me the time flashed past in joy-filled minutes. How I wished I could have stayed on that soft Atlantic swell until all the problems behind and in front of us had disappeared into oblivion, but that was not to be. Before we knew what was happening, the mountain I was heading for started to loom high over us. Later I was to learn that this massive flat-topped monster was called "Montana Roja", "Red Mountain", an extinct volcano.

'Where do you think we ought to make for?' I shouted down to the other two, after checking the dwindling reserves of petrol in the tank. 'We're running out of fuel fast, and I'm not sure we have enough to make it much farther.'

Between us we decided that the best thing to do would be to beach the yacht in a secluded spot away from any curious eyes, then scarper inland looking for provisions. I would have preferred to make for the little port that the ferry to and from Fuerteventura and Lanzarote sailed from, but it would have been too risky. I did not know if there was a harbour master, or if the theft of the yacht had been reported in Corralejo, alerting the authorities.

I sailed down the coast a little looking for a decent beach to run the boat up on. I spotted one and turned in towards it. I cut the revs as we got closer to the shore and asked Paul to jump up on the bow and keep an eye out for anything under the surface I could not see.

Too late I heard the cry of:

'Rocks!'

I flung the tiller to starboard, away from Paul's frantic gesturing to port. With a horrible grating sound the boat scraped along the side of a semi-submerged rock before hitting another completely submerged one farther on. The yacht tipped precariously and hung sideways on for a slight second, almost politely waiting for the three of us to jump for it before she capsized.

I was in the water as the yacht crashed down beside my head. The frantic high pitched screaming of the propeller as it came clear of the water then sliced down back into it a matter of inches from my head motivated my determination to get to dry land as quickly as possible. On the beach we stood on the sand dripping wet, looking at the forlorn sight of the yacht bouncing and bobbing on the tidal swell with equally forlorn hearts. It was a major setback. If we had been able to beach the yacht we could have gone looking for supplies and fuel, and attempted to make our way farther around the island.

It also looked like I could not have picked a worse place to run aground either. There was a major road running adjacent to the beach. It was almost invisible from the sea, which was why I never noticed it earlier. Thankfully there was no sign of any vehicles yet, but a half-sunken yacht would be sure to attract the attention of passers-by, from then on it would only be a matter of time before the police turned up and everyone started to put two and two together.

We weighed up our options.

We could take the road in either direction, but that was a risky strategy. Three men, two of them in Legión uniforms - albeit wet and ragged Legión uniforms - wandering along a road on an island we had no right being on in the first place was a ridiculous thought to entertain. We would not have got more than a mile before being lifted. The yacht was now completely out of the question. There was only one way, and that was up.

With a collective sigh we turned and looked up at the distant top of Montana Roja. It was a hell of a long way up, and steep, maybe five or six hundred metres at something close to a forty-degree angle. What made it worse was that we were already into our third day without anything to eat and only a couple of litres of water drunk between us in the whole time. All the same we did not waste our time, and the rate we ascended the mountain would have had our training company sergeants beaming with pride in more illustrious circumstances.

When we eventually paused to look back, a matter of metres from the top, careful not to outline ourselves against the sky, we could see that a number of cars had stopped to investigate the wreckage.

'They probably think that someone has drowned,' I said.

'Where's your jacket,' Paul asked José, pointing annoyingly at his jacket-less torso.

José closed his eyes and grimaced. He did not need to tell us what that meant. A Legión jacket had been left on the yacht, and now we only had a very short time before the regular authorities informed the military police that we were now on Lanzarote. All our hard work at getting unseen off the island was probably to no avail.

Completely knackered by this time, we once again found a small weather worn cave to hide out in and to discuss our options.

'We need money, food and water,' Paul said. 'I am the only one with civilian clothes, so it makes sense for me to make my way down to the harbour village. With a bit of luck I can find a tourist who I can borrow some money from, at least enough to phone home and get some money wired through. Hopefully I can borrow enough to get us some provisions. If we don't drink soon we'll be good for nothing.'

It was the only plan that made any sense, so once again Paul set off on his travels.

I waited in the cave with José. After a few hours he started to get jumpy.

'I will go and see if he is coming back,' he said.

I tried to talk him out of it, but he was insistent. We did not need him prowling around outside as well as Paul, and I was angry that he had decided to clear off on his own.

Once again I wondered at José's motivation. There was something wrong with him that I could not quite put my finger on. The other day on the beach when we had been waiting for Paul to come back from his recon into Corralejo, I had asked him what he would do when he got to England.

'I have some friends, some relatives. They should give me somewhere to stay,' he had replied, 'but I will be an illegal immigrant. I don't have British nationality.'

Only now did I wonder how he would obtain any travel documents without British nationality. You needed a passport to travel from Spain to England. Paul and I could apply for temporary passports from the British Consul, but José, because of his Spanish nationality, could not. He must have realised this, and the more I thought about it, the more I decided that José was working to his own schedule.

After a few more hours waiting in the silence I decided to have a look around outside myself. I climbed down into the crater and had a walk around. It was a strangely fertile place in what was otherwise such a barren landscape, probably because it caught whatever rainwater happened to fall in its naturally shaped bowl. I seem to remember coarse grass and hard-looking purple flowers. I looked out over the other side of the crater where there were a few white villas dotted around. Maybe I could find an empty one and hide out in that for a few days until the heat died down?

I decided against it. We were in this together and we had to see it through together. We had got off the island, which was no mean feat, considering the fact that we had no money, food or civilian clothes and only a hare-brained plan to work with. I concluded that we had a good chance of succeeding if Paul could find someone to lend him a little money.

A short time later, José made his way back. He appeared furtive, but that was nothing new. Back in the cave we waited for Paul. We did not have long to wait. We heard his voice shouting down to us from the crater rim an hour or two later.

'I'm sorry lads, it's all over,' he said. 'The police are with me, I got caught down in the village.'

My heart sank. This was it - the end of the road.

Cautiously we looked out of our cave. Above us we could see Paul in handcuffs flanked by three plain clothed men holding semi-automatic pistols. I recognised one of them as a military policeman I had seen around the camp back in Puerto Del Rosario.

'If you attempt to run we will shoot,' one of them shouted.

There was no escape. We were bang to rights.

Slowly we made our way up to where they were standing. Once there, we had handcuffs put on and were bundled into the back of a Land Rover. Thankfully we did not get the beating I was expecting.

'What happened?' I asked Paul as the police congratulated themselves outside as they had a smoke.

'I made it down to the village fine, and I was just in the process of persuading an English bloke to lend me some money. Initially he didn't believe the story; it took ages to convince him. He was just reaching into his wallet when the police turned up. At first there was only one of them, a youngster. I had just about convinced him that I was a German tourist and that he had got the wrong man, when the sergeant turned up. He recognised me instantly.'

We all sank into silence. José was the first to break it.

'They might be overruled by the civilian authorities,' he said hopefully. 'We were caught on Lanzarote, they might decide to deal with us here.'

'No chance,' I replied. 'Can you imagine the military police giving us up, or the colonel? They will take us back to Fuerteventura for punishment. They will want their pound of flesh.'

Once in the back of the Land Rover we were driven in the opposite direction to the port. José started to wonder again whether he was right and we were going to be dealt with by the civilian authorities. I was still confident that we would not be let off the hook that easily, and my guess was correct. We were informed that we had missed the last ferry back, and that we were going to spend the night in the cells at a guardhouse in the local regular army barracks. The sergeant giving us the information then gleefully gave a wicked smile as he raised his right hand to make a chopping motion as he sucked air in over his tobacco-stained teeth, leaving us in no doubt as to what to expect when we got back to the Tercio.

Eventually we arrived at the regular army barracks, and as the door closed on the cell at the guardhouse we settled back on our bunks to quietly ponder our fate. José was still trying to convince himself that because we had committed civilian offences, the Legión would not be allowed to administer its own particular brand of justice, but by this time I do not think that even he believed it himself. We had to be made an example of; it was the only way the colonel would be able to send the right message to the rest of the Tercio. I felt convinced that we were going to spend a long time in the work section; and that was a scary prospect. Pelotón was hard, it had to be. Ordinary life for a legionario was hard, so the punishment given to those who stepped out of line had to be a whole lot harder.

This was it. Our worst nightmare was starting to unfold upon us like a tsunami. There was no shadow of a doubt in our minds; when we got back to the barracks we were going to be in for one of the hardest times in our lives.

CHAPTER NINE

Pelotón

El Espíritu Del Pelotón De Castigo:
Sufrir Arresto En El Pelotón De Castigo Es El Derecho Del Legionario
Que Peca Militarmente, Derecho Del Cual No Debe Sustraerse Ni Por
Indulto Ni Atenuante, Pues Cuanto Más Exactamente Cumpla Su
Condena, Más De Desliga De La Falta Que Cometió.

The Spirit of Pelotón and Punishment:
To suffer arrest in 'Pelotón' and to be punished is the right of every
legionario that serves militarily, it is a right that cannot be taken from
him either by an amnesty or by extenuating circumstances, it is
important for him to complete his sentence in order to distance himself
from his previous lack of duty.

From the moment we were loaded into the Land Rovers that morning, all the way to the dock and onto the ferry, I do not remember any of us speaking a single word. Instead, we spent these last few moments of relative quiet attempting to come to terms with our fate. It is hard to describe the feelings I had then. It was as if my whole insides were being scraped out with a spoon as my heart was slowly squeezed by the giant fist of anxiety. It was the stress of knowing that something terrible was going to happen and there was nothing I could do about it. It was a feeling of complete impotence, where all options that might be able to alleviate the coming pain were searched for, yet found nowhere.

It was a time to come to terms with the fact that I had committed the crime, and now I was going to have to accept the consequences of my actions, but nothing I used to comfort myself in those moments worked. Nothing could staunch the flow of misery that swamped me. This was the single most difficult and dangerous situation I had ever been in, and eventually I reached the conclusion that the only person I could blame was myself.

Once again I had blown it. Once again, with a perverse and mad recklessness, I had wasted the opportunities that had presented themselves to me. What the hell was wrong with me? This was not normal, it could not be normal. I moaned inwardly as the Land Rovers headed towards the barracks and the reckoning that was due. My life had been a car crash up until I had joined the Legión, when things had momentarily turned around. Yet now, because I had no self-control and no common sense, I had turned the best thing to happen to me in years into a waking nightmare.

I had been handcuffed to a young military policeman who obviously took pity on me, managing to secure me a coffee and a cigarette on the ferry. I could see sympathy in his eyes, and for that I was grateful. He did not try to ease my suffering though; that would have been pointless; there were no words of sufficient comfort available. We both knew what was going to happen back at the Tercio, although he did tell me that they were very impressed with the way we had conducted our escape.

'It must have taken a lot of planning,' he said, probably hoping for a bit of information he could use.

I nodded my head and attempted a smile. I did not have the heart to tell him what a cock-up the whole thing had been from start to finish. Instead I smoked what was probably going to be my last cigarette for a long time, and watched Lanzarote and the massive Montana Roja disappear into the background. Previously I had enjoyed the trip between the two islands on the yacht, now I felt like a dead man walking. Watching the last few days travel unravel and replay backwards in front of my eyes was a poignant and sobering occasion.

When we landed at Corallejo harbour we were hurriedly thrown into the back of the Land Rovers and driven at speed back to Puerto Del Rosario. I thought that I saw a number of landmarks from when we had walked the route, mental mementos of a time that seemed so distant to me now. Still none of us spoke. The silence was palpable and said more about what we were thinking than any words could have.

Finally we entered Puerto Del Rosario, where before long the large frontage of the principal gate loomed up ominously before us. The Land Rovers screeched to a halt before the sentry on duty. We were manhandled out and frogmarched into the duty officer's room just below the arch, but not before we had caught a glimpse of the Brigada of the Pelotón standing farther back in the arch, licking his lips like the cat that had got the cream. Lined up in the office, the officer in command of the guard thumped each one of us hard in the solar plexus to get our attention. When we had got our breath back he told us what was going to happen.

'The colonel is coming to see you three cowards,' he hissed. 'If one of you moves a muscle, or even breathes funny I will beat you so badly your own mothers will not recognise you.'

Obediently we stood to attention, our faces fixed at that point in the middle distance soldiers the world over become so adept at viewing. After a minute or so the barracks resounded to the cry:

'Puerto Principal... El Coronel!'

The colonel was taller than I expected, a good few inches higher than my six foot. He carried an authoritative aristocratic air about with him, probably the result of years of being obeyed as if he was God incarnate. He was also very, very angry; no one could deny the harsh fire of fury radiating from his eyes as he walked irritably up and down in front of us.

He pointed his swagger stick at each of us individually, struggling for the words to convey what his eyes were already telling us.

'You have disgraced the Legión, your company and me, and now,' he said, 'you are going to know what it is to suffer.'

He summoned the brigada, who promptly dashed into the office.

'I want you,' he said to the brigada as he pointed to the three of us, 'to work these three scum to within an inch of their lives. I want you to break their backs the old-fashioned way. Make them rue the day they decided to disgrace the uniform they were so privileged to wear. They are to be shown no respect and no pity. Is that completely understood?'

'Yes, sir,' the brigada replied, his face fixed with a grim smile as he continued. 'No need to worry about that, sir. I'll make them wish they had never been born.'

With a last glare in our direction the colonel exited the room, leaving us in the more than capable hands of the brigada. This was the first time I had been this close to the bogey man of the Third Tercio, and I was amazed at the malevolence that emanated from him. He was a man so used to violence it seemed as if he had become a physical manifestation of it. He was a truly scary individual and I knew instinctively that there was no give in him, and certainly no mercy.

He looked each one of us in the eye for a while, daring us to challenge him. It felt like he was a powder keg waiting to go off, outwardly hoping that we would give him the reason to explode in our faces. He then hit each one of us around the face with the flat of his hand as hard as he could. He did it slowly and methodically, watching us, seeing if we would flinch, sniffing us for weakness or fear the way a predator sizes up its next meal. It was a monumental slap, succeeding in knocking me backwards as if I weighed no more than a child.

'Do not move when I hit you,' he said, 'do not even blink I will continue hitting you until we have this understanding.'

Being hit in the face is a hard thing to cope with; it strikes at the very core of your soul. When you are attacked one of the first things you do is to roll into a ball and cover your face. You do it because your face is where you are the weakest. Everything that matters is experienced through it, yet he was expecting us to be hit without even blinking.

I then realised, with a terrible certainty, what he was doing. It was an epiphany of diabolical and frightening reasoning, yet right there and then it made complete sense, and this revelation was to be one of the things that sustained me through the dark and violent months that were to come.

'You are in my power now,' he was saying without words as he hit us, 'and you will take the punishment I give you without complaint. If you do complain, or fail to surrender to my rule, I will beat you until you do. I am claiming jurisdiction over your souls and you will relinquish them to me without any preamble whatsoever.'

Undoubtedly in his eyes, flinching or not was the barometer by which he gauged whether we feared him more than our own emotions, and he would not be satisfied until he knew for certain that he was the dominant partner in the relationship. Understanding this was the means by which I was able to surrender outwardly.

In the coming weeks and months I was to see many men crack under the despotic rule of the brigada and his regime. Only my realisation prevented me from joining them. All he needed was an outward display of submission, and I was obviously going to have to give him that if I wanted to survive. However, I resolved there and then that I was not going to lay myself down to die. Inwardly I was determined to resist. I am from stubborn Yorkshire stock; my outward obedience would cover my inward rebellion.

'No man,' I inwardly told myself, 'is going to get the best of me.'

Yet just saying that was not going to save my hide. The trick was going to be making sure that the brigada did not know that I was still my own man, and the only way I was going to convince him of that was to do everything I was told to do, quickly, professionally and without any outward manifestation of the fact that I was keeping hold of what was the only thing I had left - my self-will and my pride.

It was improbable that he consciously understood what he was doing in that first mental battle between us. He was almost certainly self-taught in the ways of repression and authoritarianism. I could not imagine him taking a degree in psychology, or reading any books on psychoanalysis in order to become a better prison warden.

Later someone told me that the brigada had spent so long in Pelotón as a prisoner they decided to make him a guard. It was almost certainly not true. He would never have made brigada if he was constantly in trouble, but in a weird and wonderful way it made complete sense. If he had spent time as a prisoner himself he had learnt his craft the best possible way. He understood how to treat prisoners because he had been one himself. He was merely doing his job as he understood it, how he had been taught. It was nothing personal, and when I understood this it all made sense. Like everything in the code of Legión brutality, it was merely the way things were done because that's how they were done.

When he came to me and pulled his hand back to strike me again, I did not move. I stared straight ahead and forced myself to stay still. It is hard to do, very hard, especially when you had just had a taste of how strong the man was, but it was necessary. This was a tutorial we had to learn. The other two must have understood this at the same time as me, because he grunted approval at our reaction to the next blow before ordering us outside. We had passed the first lesson.

Two lance corporals were waiting for us in the arch. Ominously they both carried truncheons. It was the first time I had ever seen a Pelotón guard carrying such a weapon. Wooden truncheons had supposedly been banned ever since a prisoner had been beaten to death in the seventies. This did not bode well for us at all. We were then ordered at double time up to the Pelotón fort.

The white-walled edifice came into view as the guards behind us hurried on up with prods in the back and slaps around the back of the head. Inside we came upon our welcoming committee, another half a dozen lance corporals, each one of them was also carrying a truncheon.

I cannot say that the beating did not hurt because it did, but strangely it did not hurt as much as I had expected it to, a small fact that I was able to find some comfort in as they laid into me. Maybe there were too many of them and they got in each other's way, I don't really know, but it was a sustained assault, and to protect myself I did what everyone does in such circumstances; I rolled up into a ball on the floor and waited for them to stop.

As the blows rained down I wondered when the blow would land that would break a bone or render me unconscious. Mercifully that blow never came, and after what seemed like an age, but was probably no more than a minute, we were ordered back onto our feet.

Hurting all over and barely able to stand, we fixed our eyes at the middle distance and attempted to come to attention.

'That,' said the brigada, patrolling up and down in front of us with a fierce glare in his eyes and spittle flying in our faces as he spat out the words, 'is just a taste of what you will get if you put one foot out of line during your residency here.'

We were then thrown into the dog kennels, small holding cells a mere three feet wide by five feet high and six feet long. I nearly gagged as I first entered. They stank terribly, because when not in use by prisoners they housed the assortment of guard dogs that made the fort their home. There were no creature comforts. The doors were heavy steel with a slide-back grill that was used by the guards to check up on us. The walls were cold concrete, and there was no blanket, to make it worse there was no light or sound inside after the door was slammed shut. Not even a miserly chink of daylight or a lone solitary sound was able to make its comforting way in. You had no way of knowing whether it was the middle of the day or night.

Alone in the darkness, and unable to stand properly because of the lack of headroom, I sat down, hoping to God that the dogs had left behind nothing more than their smell. Gingerly I checked myself for any wound or injury. Thankfully I could feel nothing other than some tender spots that might prove troublesome in the morning as they bruised and tightened up the muscles. I then attempted to come to terms with my incarceration in what was nothing more than a concrete tomb.

Being isolated in complete darkness is a strange thing to happen to you, sensory deprivation is quite uniquely debilitating. It gradually and determinedly robs you of your confidence. So much of what we make of the world is experienced through the gifts of sight and sound, and when you are robbed of both, you slowly enter a world where nothing makes much sense any more except what is going on in your head, and after a while even that starts to lead you astray.

Your thoughts, because they are the only things you can "see" and "hear" in the darkness end up becoming your reality, and then, if you are not careful, your living nightmare. The voice you initially listen to is obviously yourself, your companion in the claustrophobic enclave, but after only a short while it starts to become disjointed, detached from your own ability to rein it in. It becomes something uncontrolled, and quite incredibly scary.

Sleep did not help either. I remember my dreams being vivid. Not the sedate black and white ones of a normal night-time tryst, but the vibrant colour-filled ones that wake you up drenched in sweat as they reach their unpleasant crescendo. They were of the type that left me breathless and palpitating in their lucid afterglow. I tried to read them, wondering what divine portent was hidden in the kaleidoscope of colour that had momentarily gripped my subconscious, but there was never anything of comfort there. Only the dark remembrance of my incarceration to welcome me back to consciousness, and it was a painful thing in those few momentary seconds, to feel the fine-grained sands of hope that were supposed to welcome my wakefulness slowly slip through my fingers.

It was late morning when we were slammed up in the kennels, and but for a couple of small meals of soup, bread and water that we were forced to eat standing up at the door of our cells, we were kept locked up for the rest of that day and another night. I began to wonder whether this was going to be permanent, and prayed to God that it would not be. I could not imagine hanging onto my sanity for much longer in such circumstances.

*

After breakfast the morning of the third day, instead of being thrown back into the cells, the three of us were ordered into line by the main gate. The brigada once again made sure that we were compliant by thumping each of us in the stomach hard before ordering the gate open. To our dismay we saw the whole barracks formed up before us. We were then ordered to walk in a circle in full view of all the legionarios on parade as the officers of the respective companies explained to their men that this was what would happen to them if they ever dared to desert.

That walk of shame was probably one of the most humiliating things I have ever been forced to do in my whole life. It was a calculated act designed to publicly debase us, and it worked. I felt like a pariah. How I wished in those moments that I could have gone back in time to prevent myself from absconding. If I could have time-travelled, instead of being here disgraced before the whole Tercio, I would have been looking on from the safety of the ranks at Paul and José as they did their walk of shame. However, that was nothing more than a fantasy, all I had was the reality, and only God Himself knew how wretched I felt then.

We must have looked and smelled terrible. We had barely eaten in a week, we had certainly not bathed or shaved, and our uniforms were torn and unkempt. I did not know what my own face looked like after the beatings, but if Paul and José's lumps and bruises were anything to go by I looked a mess.

If the legionarios watching needed proof that we had been nothing more than a trio of idiots, then they had their confirmation in full view. We had attempted something that, if it had succeeded, would have gone down in the folklore of our own remembrance for the rest of our lives, instead we had been caught, and now our names would live forever in infamy, especially in the memory of those with whom we served. We had become exactly what the colonel wanted us to be, a salutary lesson in the consequences of gross stupidity and a severe warning to others who might have been planning anything similar.

Having completed our public humiliation, the heavy metal gate of Pelotón closed behind us, and I do not think that any prisoner alive would have been more pleased to see the inside of the work section as I was in that moment - but my relief was short-lived.

'Now,' the brigada declared with an evil smile, 'you are going to sweep the parade ground, but first we will take you out of those uniforms you have disrespected and put you in something more fitting your new station in life.'

That can't be right, I thought, sweeping the parade ground sounded too easy.

Three blue boiler suits were then thrown at us, and under a hail of blows we were ordered to undress and put them on. In the place of our shoes we got second hand green trainers, and for our heads, second hand Legión Chapiris with the trademark red tassel ripped off. There was to be no objection about anything given, and I dared not mention that the trainers I had been given were obviously too small for me.

The change into prison dress was more poignant for me than anything else that happened in those few days. It reinforced permanently on my psyche how far I had fallen from grace. I remembered how proud I was when I had first dressed myself in my new Legión uniform in Ronda. How pleased I was to have been allowed into the hallowed ranks of "La Legión Española". Yet now, here I was, wearing a mockery of the uniform, a man with no honour, a man who did not deserve any honour, and I felt that sense of shame acutely. Yet no amount of breast beating or mourning would change my circumstances. I had erred, and now I was going to suffer the punishment that Legión discipline dictated.

I resolved there and then to accept the punishment given as apt for my crimes, and although I had previously resolved to remain my own man - something I knew was fundamentally important for my own mental welfare - I would, nevertheless, submit to the yoke of my sentence willingly and without complaint. I would not deny the Legión its pound of flesh. Maybe then, I hoped I would be able to expunge the shame of my crime and salvage some honour from this whole catastrophe.

I knew that it was a thankless undertaking. Who could I possibly go to and say, 'I went AWOL, but I suffered silently in my punishment, working hard and without complaint at every task given me, thereby redeeming some honour'? No one would listen; no one would be interested in how I conducted myself now, only me. However, it was the only option left open to me, the only way I could silently offer atonement to the regiment that had taken me in when no one else wanted me, gave me a home and a family when I had not got one, and given me a purpose in life when I was so completely adrift.

It was not much to offer, but it was all I had.

After we had changed we were left alone for a short while as the brigada passed onto the corporal on duty exactly what was expected of us. During this moment I was able to survey in more detail our new home.

The inner sanctum of "Sección De Trabajo" was a rectangular courtyard internally. Apart from a water tank enclosed in whitewashed breeze block sited in the middle of the open courtyard, all the living accommodation, eating area, cells, toilets, stores and offices were set against the walls. It was clean, with an air of rapid efficiency about everything that happened. This was to be my home for heaven alone knew how long, and as alien and violent as it was, I was going to have to learn the ropes sooner rather than later.

A whack around the head brought me back from my appraisal.

'Go and get a bucket and brush each,' a particularly skinny and ancient-looking corporal said, pointing to a store situated along the back wall.

He was one of the permanent corporals, a team of five under the brigada, who worked exclusively in the Pelotón. Beneath these there were three full-time lance corporals and a team of lance corporals on secondment from their companies. Apart from one corporal, who smoked a pipe and looked like he should have been wearing slippers with grandchildren bouncing up and down on his knee, they were all of a particularly vicious temperament and appeared to me to be complete lunatics.

Thankfully we knew exactly what he meant. We had seen the prisoners often enough around camp carrying their blue buckets and reed hand-held brushes, as they traversed the camp collecting the litter and cigarette ends so casually dropped by those who did not have to pick them up. It did not look like hard work, and once again I wondered why we had been given such light work at the start of our incarceration. I would have expected something much harder. After we had collected the utensils, we were marched at the double out of the gate and down towards the parade ground.

The parade ground itself was about the size of a football field and paved with heavy granite slabs. To one end was the main gate, and at the other was the Legión cenotaph where a pillar stood, on holy days it had fixed upon it the plaster cast model of a crucified Christ. At the base of the column were the busts of famous legionarios including Franco and Milan Astray, the two founders of the Legión. On the wall behind the column the battle honours of the Legión were emblazed on a large brass plaque, which recounted the famous battles and wars in which the Legión had engaged, and the number of "glorious" dead in each. To the other sides were the barracks of the Caballería, along with the chapel and the legionarios' bar.

My initial scepticism at how easy our first task was going to be was confirmed when it was explained to us by the corporal guarding us that we were not to sweep normally. Instead we were to sweep it with our body held at a ninety-degree angle to our legs. To make matters worse we were informed that we were not allowed to bend our legs or rest our hands upon our knees. One hand was to be behind our back at all times, and we were to keep our eyes fixed firmly on the ground.

'The colonel is watching,' the corporal said, a trace of mock sympathy inflecting his words, 'and this is how he is going to make sure that your backs are indeed broken.'

Stupidly I hazarded a look upwards at the rooms situated above the arch at the main gate where the colonel lived. I could see nothing, and was rewarded with a blow to the back of my head for my impudence.

'Keep your head down,' the corporal hissed. 'Prisoners are not allowed to look another legionario in the eye, they must not speak unless spoken to and they most certainly do not look up. Your eyes will be fixed firmly on the ground at all times, and you will not stand erect until I give you permission, is that clear?'

'Si, mi cabo,' we replied in unison.

'Good, now get on with it,' he replied. 'The mood the colonel is in, if I'm seen to be giving you an easy time I'll be for the chop too. You three have managed to upset the nearest thing to God on this island, and he won't rest until you have been seen to pay the price.'

Suitably admonished we bent double and proceeded to sweep the flagstones beneath us.

After only a short while I could tell that I was not going to cope with this very well. Having been born with a dislocated hip meant that there were certain things I was unable to do, such as touch my toes, sit cross-legged and bend double at the waist in the manner I was being asked to here. I was in agony after only a few hundred yards.

It took approximately fifteen turns up and down the parade ground sweeping a flagstone's width each before we had finished. In spite of the intense pain I managed to hang on until we had done, hoping in my heart of hearts that we would be put onto something else when we had finished.

'Right,' said the corporal as we finished the last slab... 'turn around and do it again.'

Our hearts sank, and I realised with a sickening finality that I was not going to complete this punishment. Sure enough, after a short while my legs gave way as a sharp and intense stab of pain shot through my lower back. This was a "back spasm" and it had happened to me only twice before in my whole life, once when I had been forced to sit cross-legged at a school concert for over two hours, and once when lifting something too heavy for me when I was in the Merchant Navy. In basic terms the muscles in my back had contracted, rendering me completely incapable of movement. Apparently it is an involuntary protection mechanism my back muscles initiate in order to prevent serious injury to my muscles themselves, my spine or the ligaments, or so the doctor had explained to me the first time it had happened.

Lying on the floor I imagined the colonel looking out of his window and smiling down on my fallen form. He had wanted to "break my back", and now it looked like he was succeeding. I hated the mental image, and tried to get up as the humiliation I felt bit deep into me, but even a few blows with the truncheon followed by a couple of kicks from our cursing corporal could not persuade my temporarily inflexible body to move.

'Get up,' Paul and José whispered anxiously, their eyes also on the colonel's windows, 'it's just as hard for us too.'

I wanted to explain that it was not as hard for them as it was for me because thankfully they had not got the same physical ailment, but what would be the point in that? As far as they were concerned I was lining up trouble not just for myself, but for them also. Eventually, after what seemed like an age, the muscles in my back loosed slightly and I managed to get to my feet.

Every step was unremitting agony, and I found it almost impossible to put one foot in front of the other. The only thing keeping me going was the irritating mental image of the colonel thinking that he had broken me. I wanted to show him that even though my body was getting wrecked, my soul was still my own. No one had ever beaten me in that regard, or were they ever going to as far as I was concerned. I was determined that I would remain defiant until I dropped down dead.

My captors might have the power of life and death over me, but they would never conquer me.

I took heart from an old Legión saying; one that had initially been told to me by an old legionario, one of the many I had come to know who had made the Legión their home. Men who carried their long service medals etched on their faces in every scar and sunburnt wrinkle, who carried a calm resignation to the suffering involved in order to bear the privilege of being a bridegroom of death.

"Los muertos no tengan el miedo de morir", "The dead have no fear of dying", he had said with a smile and a wink, just after our section had been ordered to run up this impossibly steep hill in gas masks one blisteringly hot day while on manoeuvres. He did it faster than I did as well, on a diet of hashish, cheap wine, and lentil and potato stew.

Maybe my determination to resume, but my obvious actual inability to do so, persuaded the corporal to take me seriously, because he suddenly decided that I needed to see the doctor. The doctor on duty was obviously very concerned about my back. After he had examined me and given me an oral painkiller, he was in the process of telling the corporal that I needed to rest when the door suddenly burst open. It was the brigada, and he looked angrier than a bear with toothache that had been woken up too early from its hibernation.

He went completely ballistic. First of all he battered me around the head a few times, sending me sprawling across a bed, then he battered Paul and José, finally he gave the corporal a whack that nearly floored him. The doctor, a lieutenant, backed away in terror, probably imagining that he was going to be next, but I honestly think that Attilla the Hun would have backed away from the brigada at that precise moment. His rage was truly bestial in its ferocity.

'What the hell is happening?' the brigada shouted, barely able to speak because he was so incensed. 'I have just had the colonel on the phone asking why you aren't out there sweeping.'

Good tactic, I thought, batter first, ask questions later.

The doctor, probably remembering that he was the senior officer present stepped forwards.

'This prisoner,' he said pointing to me, 'was brought to me with what appears to be a severe back problem. I was just in the process-'

'He's faking,' the brigada interrupted.

'In my medical opinion-'

'I'm telling you, sir,' the brigada interrupted again, stepping forwards until he was merely inches from the poor doctor's face, spittle flying from his lips, 'that he is faking.'

It was well known in the Legión that to avoid work in Pelotón as a prisoner, you had to have a very visible injury that everyone agreed exempted you from work, or no pulse. Anything invisible to the naked eye was obviously not painful because it could not be seen.

'Then if you are so convinced that he is faking, I will insist that you sign a release form taking full responsibility for any injury that may happen to this prisoner if you send him back to work.'

Thank God for the Hippocratic oath, I thought.

I could see the brigada's brain cells whirring away behind his angry little eyes. If he signed the form and something happened to me then he would be liable in spite of what the colonel had ordered. Senior officers the world over have a Teflon-based ability to avoid culpability for anything that goes wrong, and the uncanny ability to sweep up the medals when it goes right. However, the brigada also knew that if he did not get me back to work soon, he would suffer the full wrath of the colonel.

'Then you give me a form that releases him from work,' he finally said to the doctor. 'Something I can present to the colonel to keep him off my back.'

He turned to glare at me accusingly, and my heart did a somersault at the thought of the retribution coming my way.

'How long are you going to sign him off for?' the brigada asked.

'A couple of days should do it,' the doctor replied.

I thought the brigada would explode in response to the doctor's suggestion. His face went bright purple and his hands started to shake. He was about to launch into another tirade in the doctor's hapless face, when I said something so incredibly stupid I did not realise that I was saying it until the words were actually coming out of my mouth. It was almost as if my brain had heard what I was thinking of saying, but because it did not believe that I would be so unutterably idiotic as to speak them out loud, it did not stop me.

'I will be all right in an hour or so,' I said. 'It has happened to me before. All I need to do is lay down flat for a short while until my muscles stop their spasm.'

Later I thought about what I had said and why. I decided that such an insane outburst was probably prompted by my previous determination to suffer honourably, and getting signed off for something that will have gone in an hour did not match the masochistic criteria I had set myself. Even after saying it I was mentally cursing myself for being a complete idiot.

The brigada, who had stepped forwards as if to hit me for having the gall to speak before I had been spoken to, froze in mid-strike. His brain was certainly being put through its paces this morning, as once again I could see his eyes reflecting the frantic computations my comment had initiated. He lowered his hand, his face having decided to settle on a puzzled expression.

'In an hour you will be fit enough to go back to sweeping?'

'Si, mi brigada,' I replied, inwardly cursing my stubborn determination, I had been seconds away from at least a day on my back.

A sly look passed across his eyes.

'Then you admit that you were faking?'

'No, sir,' I replied. 'If I had been faking I would have taken the doctor up on his offer of three days rest.'

The puzzled look became even more puzzled as he opened and closed his mouth a few times before deciding on his solution.

'Take them back to the compound for something to eat,' he said to the corporal before turning to leave. 'He can have an hour, but he is not to lie down, he remains standing, is that understood?'

The corporal, who was still rubbing his jaw after the massive blow he had received from the ham-fisted brigada, nodded his head.

On the way back to the fort I was cursed by Paul for being a fool.

'You are a complete nutter,' Paul said, 'what idiot passes up bed rest?'

José merely sniggered in disbelief.

The corporal behind us told them to shut up, and walked us in silence back up the hill to Pelotón.

Inside we were fed, and I was pleased to see that at least the portions were not measly. It would have been impossible to maintain our current level of exertion without enough sustenance to fuel our bodies.

It was our first time in the common eating area, and we were not in the least bit surprised to see that there were no chairs, only two long tables around which blue boiler-suited prisoners ate their food from metal trays on the table in front of them while standing up. Prisoners were not allowed to sit down, ever. It was strictly forbidden. The only time they were able to take the load off their feet was when they went to sleep at night.

It was a spartan room, the only adornment being the Spirit of Pelotón hand painted almost lovingly on one of the walls. I took quick glances at my fellow prisoners as I ate. To a man they looked knackered and world-weary. Normal punishment was fifteen days, and after such a short time it was known for men to lose between seven to ten kilos, well over seventeen pounds in weight. More serious offences could carry a thirty-day sentence, and the physical exertions had been known to kill some. I wondered what term we would get, certainly not less than thirty days.

After eating we were formed up outside in the sun and stood at ease.

It is a strange thing to stand in the sun with a bellyful of food. Your brain and body tell you that it is time to nap, but your inability to do so means that you fall asleep for a microsecond before you stumble, and as soon as you do stumble, because that is inevitable, you are whacked by one of the corporals standing guard over you. It was a bit of a game to them, taking bets as to who would close their eyes first.

In between trying to stay awake and blows to the head I heard two of the corporals talking. One of them was the skinny guy who had been guarding us on the parade ground.

'Is that him?' his mate was asking, nodding his head in my direction.

Our corporal nodded.

'I have never seen the brigada flummoxed like that, ever.'

They both shook their heads in amazement as I pretended not to be listening.

'Do you think he's mad?'

'I'm not sure,' our corporal replied, 'he is English though.'

'We're going to have to watch him, he's potential trouble.'

I smiled to myself. I had scored my first point. I was unsure what the point was, or how I had scored it, but I felt better about myself, much better. The feeling lasted until we were ordered to collect our buckets and reed brushes, and make our way back to the parade ground. From then on until the sun started to dip towards the horizon, I was once again in a whole world of pain.

CHAPTER TEN

Digging the Cesspit

Mathew 10:28
*Do not be afraid of those who kill the body but cannot kill the soul.
Rather, be afraid of the One who can destroy both soul and body in
hell.*

The sweeping of the parade ground carried on for another day and a half, after which the colonel probably got tired of watching us from the window and we were assimilated into the main body of prisoners. Out of the spotlight we became nothing more than ordinary prisoners, and we were thankful for the fact that we were not targeted for anything more grievous than standard Pelotón living.

The first few weeks took on a familiar pattern. First thing in the morning, at around five o'clock, the door of the cell was hammered upon by whoever the on-duty corporal was. This was the cue to get up, and like everything else in Legión life, it was to be done fast.

If we were fortunate we had got to bed before midnight the previous day, if not it could have been one o'clock before we were banged up for the night. We slept communally, up to thirty of us in a large rectangular concrete cell. After a while we did not notice the stench, but anyone who entered and was not prepared for the aroma of thirty unwashed sweaty bodies was often knocked back on their heels.

We slept on one-inch thick, dirty, yellow foam mattresses, under an equally dirty blanket, no pillows were provided. Most of us rolled up our boiler suit and used that to rest our head upon. There was one door, a huge metal thing made of solid steel, and one window with no glass and three separate tiers of metal bars solidly built into the wall to prevent any thought of escape. In the corner was a hole in the ground that was our toilet, modesty was catered for by a small wall beside it that only just shielded you from public view.

By far the best part of the day was when the door was closed, the bars thrown and the locks snapped shut. This was when we laid ourselves down to sleep. It was bliss to lay our aching bodies down, and for a few seconds, before the quick onset of sleep, we knew a small transitory moment of pleasure. Every other moment of our long day was watched and scrutinised, this was the only moment we had to ourselves, and we drank it up, hoping as our eyes surrendered to sleep that our dreams would transport us to a place of rest and refreshment.

Unfortunately the enjoyment of our dreams was cruelly decimated when the door was loudly banged on to indicate that we had at least thirty seconds to get up, put on our boiler suits and trainers, and throw our mattresses onto a pile in the corner. God help any prisoner who failed to be ready when the door was finally thrown open. If someone was not standing in line, this was the cue for the first beating of the day.

On one occasion, a black legionario who had been sent here for some misdemeanour he vehemently declared to not having committed, failed to get himself ready when the door opened. It was his first morning, and he had unwisely decided that a "go-slow" was the best way to protest his innocence. We warned him that his actions would have severe consequences on his physical health, but he chose not to listen. Unfortunately for him it was a bad-tempered fellow African who opened the door, a corporal with a reputation for never smiling, never cutting any slack, and having a punch almost equal in power to the brigada himself.

I will never forget how the ferocity of the attack produced a look of complete terror on the poor lad's face, until eventually one particularly vicious punch rendered him completely unconscious. I remember feeling vaguely guilty about my lack of empathy towards the unconscious soldier. I had viewed the whole incident with the cruel and dispassionate air of someone who did not really care what happened to those around me; and a small voice inside threw out a mild and barely heard cry of scorn at the man I had become.

The next morning, complete with black eye and fat lip he was the first one ready in line. Pelotón was good at that. It taught you to respect and obey the system. I never saw it engender anything except obedience in even the hardest man to put on the boiler suit. Everyone was brought low as a prisoner; there was no royalty, and no exceptions.

Outside in the mild predawn twilight we were lined up and sectioned off into different groups. The main activity of this first part of the day was to collect any rubbish and cigarette ends around the camp, using the blue buckets and reed brushes. Some were sent to the communal toilets in order to get them ready for inspection, a particularly odious task if it was after a Friday or Saturday night payday. A few others were retained in the fort for cleaning duties, but the majority of us were sent out litter picking. It seemed to be important to show the rest of the barracks that the Pelotón went to bed after everybody else, and were up and about before everyone else was awake.

These mornings were often a reflective time and, depending on the corporal guarding you, could be somewhat peaceful. All the lance corporals, bar three lunatics who were permanent, were on secondment to the Pelotón from their companies, and most hated it. They knew full well that within a few hours of getting sent back to their companies they could be sent back as prisoners for even a minor misdemeanour, and God help any man who had been too heavy-handed as a guard when the cell door was locked for the night and him on the wrong side of the door. Knowing this, and the fact that sometimes one or two of the lads they were guarding were mates from their own company, the lance corporals might try to find a hidden corner where they would let us sit down and have a cigarette. They might even let us roll a joint if one of us was fortunate enough to have some hashish, and they were brave enough.

I was constantly amazed as to how much contraband we were able to get hold of as prisoners. Friends and dealers would pass it on to us by various and increasingly imaginative means. Cigarettes would be thrown down in front of us that we then swept up and, when no one was looking, concealed somewhere on our person. I became quite adept at sleight of hand. Once, just before lock-up, I was strip-searched by four guards looking for a packet of cigarettes they knew I had, ones they wanted because they had run out. I managed to avoid getting them confiscated by constantly moving the packet to various parts of my body and clothing seemingly under full view. I discovered that getting away with such things is often all about misdirection and brazen confidence.

Hashish was likewise dropped or placed in various hidey-holes for us to collect long after the colleague or dealer had hidden it for us. Some guards themselves would sell us a strip of hashish for a promise of payment at an inflated price when we had access to our pay back in our companies later. On one occasion we even managed to get hold of a bottle of brandy, but that was a mistake; working in the sun under the influence of alcohol was almost suicidal considering the fact that we were often badly dehydrated anyway.

Not all the lance corporals were as accommodating though. Some took their responsibilities too seriously, and unfortunately some decided that they enjoyed the power. On one occasion I was threatened with a loaded pistol by a guard I had offended.

It all happened because a call went out one morning for a volunteer for "el camión", "the lorry". The lorry was by far and away the best posting to get as a prisoner. It came with privileges and, unbeknown to me, was always offered to the longest serving prisoners who sometimes even paid for the honour by bribes. I stepped forwards as soon as I heard the word "volunteer".

In my defence, I had no idea that the lorry was a cushy number at this stage of my incarceration, or that a prisoner behind me - a friend of one of the guards - had been given the nod as the next volunteer. I took it for granted that when someone shouted out for a volunteer, you volunteered. This was standard Legión protocol. Besides, who asks for a volunteer in Pelotón when he has thirty souls at his beck and call? If you wanted someone to do something you merely ordered them to do it. I stepped up because I thought that by not volunteering I would get into trouble.

The lorry had the job of collecting the bins of rubbish situated around the camp and outside where the NCOs and officers had their quarters. The rubbish bins used were forty-gallon drums; our job was to collect the trash twice a day. There were always four prisoners and two guards on this detail. One of the guards sat in the front with the driver, the other was in the back with us. In the morning, two of us would be outside the truck running to the bins and lifting them up to the guys in the back who emptied them and passed them back down, in the afternoon we switched over. It was hard work, with the daily run somewhere in the region of eight miles by the time we had done the full round.

The trick with this detail was to get the run over with as quickly as possible because the perk came later at the rubbish dump situated on the outskirts of the town. There to meet us was a goatherd with two bottles of wine and forty cigarettes. He was after the loaves of bread and anything else we could collect for his goats to eat. On the round we assiduously collected all we could for him in a bin at the back of the truck. Upon receipt of his bread he would hand over the contraband. One bottle and twenty of the cigarettes went to the guards, the rest came to us.

After the rubbish had been shovelled out of the back of the lorry and swept clean, we were allowed a sit down, a drink and a smoke. It was bliss. The quicker we had made the run, the longer we had to rest. The rubbish was also a great place to scavenge, and our diet was often supplemented by cakes and biscuits retrieved from the waste others had thrown out. It was here that I managed to finally get rid of the trainers that were blistering my feet when I found a used pair my size.

On this occasion though, my interference in the selection process had annoyed everyone on the truck, with the guard who had attempted to secure a place for his friend getting incredibly vexed with me. So much so that at one stage he pulled out his pistol, cocked it and pointed it straight at me. He was calmed down by the other three prisoners, who explained in no uncertain terms that come the afternoon, when the detail was called again, I was to feign a hand injury, thereby allowing the lad who had been picked beforehand back on. Not wanting to start a feud, I agreed. Consequently, that afternoon I was back out sweeping.

Generally later in the day, before and after the evening meal, we were drilled in the yard, but being prisoners we were not allowed the privilege of marching in the style of the Legión, we had to do it differently. Instead of the one right hand being thrown up in front of the face as was normal when the Legión marched, both had to be. As well as this, the left foot had to be brought down with a smack onto the ground, lending the whole show a curiously fierce and lopsided aspect. It must have looked very impressive to an outsider, but in the ranks it was physically very tiring, and we were sometimes at it for hours. Many a time someone either passed out or threw up from the sheer effort of it.

The last job of the day was to clean the legionarios' bar. This was done when the rest of the barracks were getting to bed, and depending on how many of us there were in Pelotón at the time it was this activity that dictated what time we finally got to bed. Nothing was worse than being nearly dead on your feet, hearing the bugle sound lights out for everyone else and marching in column to the bar for what was going to be another hour or two of labour.

The bar was up some steps just off the parade ground and was the size of a basketball court inside. Like everything else, the cleaning was done at the double. The tables and chairs were metal and very heavy. First of all these had to be carried outside and hosed down by a water truck. Inside we first swept up all the rubbish, then mopped as the water truck hosed the floor. When everything was checked and passed as satisfactorily clean, the furniture was brought back inside. Only then were we marched back and locked up for the night.

Besides the standard cleaning duties, throughout the day any job could be sprung upon us at a moment's notice, from whitewashing buildings to filling in holes in the road. Pelotón was the remedy to any manpower shortage anywhere in the camp, and we were utilised as such. On one occasion a cement mixer broke down and four of us were assigned to mix five tonnes of cement for a footing for a new building.

We were so quick that when we left we heard the sergeant in charge of the building project telling our guard that we four had completed the job in a quarter of the time his eight workers could have done it with a mixer.

A brief respite was offered on Sundays when we were allowed to have a shower and wash our boiler suits before hanging them out to dry in the sun. It was a curiously sad sight, the blue overalls drying as we stood in formation in our underpants waiting to put them on again when dry.

Sometimes the priest also popped by for a visit, offering confession to those who requested it, and handing out inane platitudes along with a few cigarettes. His "job" done with us, he would disappear into the lance corporal's rest room before staggering out a few hours later having obviously imbibed too much wine. He was not a glowing advertisement for Christianity, and Paul and José used him as an excuse to ridicule my faith. I have to admit to watching him and wondering whether I was on the right track in my search for the truth, but I balanced it out by admitting that I was also a poor Christian, if I could even consider myself that at this sorry stage of my life.

After a few weeks of such graft I had not got a single ounce of fat on me, and my fitness levels had hit new heights. I could run and work all day, sleep for four hours, get up and do it all again, but just when I was thinking that I would be able to manage my incarceration reasonably well, we were informed by a grinning corporal that some of us were going to be assigned for "special duties" at the basic training camp the next day.

The following morning, Paul, José and I along with fifteen others were ordered to collect up all the shovels, pickaxes, sledgehammers and wheelbarrows we had in the store and load them onto a waiting lorry. This was not a good sign. The tools meant that we were in for some serious hard labour; quite how hard it was going to be I was soon to learn.

*

Up until this moment in my imprisonment I had used the time that we were working and not allowed to talk, to think. There was only one topic of thought during this time, and the question that kept coming back to haunt me time and time again was... why?

Why was I here?

What was the purpose to my life?

Was there even a purpose?

I felt like I was drowning in a sea of despair, and it was probably true to say that I struggled inwardly in all likelihood more than I did physically. My mind was a whirlpool of anger and doubt. I could find no reason for anything. I tried to remember the words I had read in the Good News Bible before I had petulantly hidden it in the bottom of my locker just because it had become too hard for me to accept what I was reading. All that kept coming back to me was the fact that I was a sinner and that I needed to be saved, but what was sin? How on earth could I be saved? What was right and wrong anyway, and what was the point in accepting the fact that I was a sinner if that fact alone did nothing other than crush me even further?

I still wanted to say that I was a follower of Christ, a disciple even, and I wanted to say it with the same conviction that the Hare Krishnas said it when they referred to themselves as "devotees of Krishna". However, I could not. Not only was I reluctant to commit myself to something I was finding it hard to imagine living like, but I also knew that I was a long way short of any mark I imagined God having set for the acceptance of anyone - a very long way. I was a thief, a drug taker and a prisoner, and I had even blown the opportunity the Legión had given me to start a new life with a clean slate. I was a complete screw up, and it seemed to me that I could get no further from God than if I physically went to Hell itself.

He must have heard me thinking, because something as close to Hell as I had ever had the misfortune to see was exactly where I went next.

*

On the journey back down to the basic training camp we were informed exactly what was in store for us. The camp was apparently in need of a large soakaway cesspit. The site had grown considerably in the last few years and the current one was overflowing. In the minds of the authorities there were two solutions to the predicament; they could hire in large bulldozers to do the job, or they could use the Pelotón. It was a no-brainer. We were there, we were cheap, and we were expendable.

We were taken to the area designated. It was a parcel of land approximately fifty metres by fifty. We had to clear away all the rocks and shrubs then remove a metre of topsoil before placing boulders collected from the area around the camp in the hole, largest on the bottom, smallest at the top. We were then going to cover it all back up with the topsoil we had previously removed. In addition, we also had to dig a large pit five metres by five, and four metres deep, this larger hole would act as the initial reservoir for the waste that would then feed the larger area.

'We have two weeks to complete this,' the brigada told us. 'I have given my word that I will be done by then, and if you prove me to be a liar I will skin you alive.'

He then handed over to two corporals. One was the skinny one who had guarded us the first day we swept the parade ground, and the other one was the old boy with the pipe. They quickly made it quite clear that the brigada's deadline would be met.

Clearing the rocks and shrubs was done in a couple of days, the removal of the topsoil a few more. The pace was relentless and the heat stifling. What made it worse was the dusty volcanic soil itself. It was like working in a sulphur factory. It got up your nose and in your hair, in your eyes and ears; it choked the life out of you. As well as this irritation to contend with, I was unused to using tools, so after the first day my hands were blistered and bleeding so badly I could barely grasp the handle of the pickaxe the following day.

One of the full-time Pelotón lance corporals noticed my discomfort and gave me some curious advice.

'Urinate on them,' he said. 'Believe me, it helps.'

I followed his advice and became a convert to this particular remedy when I saw how quickly the blisters dried and healed. After a couple of days I had no more problems with my hands - if only that had been the worst of my problems.

The pace never relented. From sun up to sun down we worked, and from that day to this I do not think that I have ever worked so hard. We were only allowed to pause if we asked for water, or when we were sent to eat. Going slow or easing up was rewarded with a beating, and only those who suffered a visible physical injury such as a broken arm or leg were removed from the detail.

Every morning, when woken by the bashing on the cell door, I had to crack loose my muscles and joints, which had seized in the night, and try from somewhere to summon up the confidence that I would see another day out without falling flat on my face or getting injured.

It was here that I cried out to God.

I do not think that previously to this moment I had ever meant anything I had ever said to God. I had toyed with prayer the way countless thousands had, and I had thought a lot about Him, eternity and the world around me, as do many millions, but I do not think that I had ever spoken directly to Him before, at least never so passionately, or so desperately wanting an answer back.

It was at the bottom of the hole that I let rip at Heaven, where I could not see my hand in front of my face for the sulphuric dust, and where we had hit a bed of solid rock that was seriously hindering our efforts. Initially we had been ordered to pickaxe through the bedrock, but many broken pickaxe handles and bad injuries later, even the guards decided that it was impossible. They then supplied us with sledgehammers and metal rods to work into the cracks, telling us to break up the solid rock as if it was no more than heavy soil.

My lungs were burning because I was trying to breathe through my nose in order to avoid sucking in mouthfuls of dust. I could barely open my eyes because they were so crusted up, and on one occasion my hands even cleaved to the sledgehammer handle through sustained use, only coming loose when a guard prised me off it digit by digit. It was hell on earth. I could not imagine being anywhere harder or more painful. Not only was I suffering physically, but I was also at my wits' end emotionally.

'You have got to prove to me that you exist,' I cried out in a sudden explosion of anger and frustration in the midst of the dust and the heat. 'If you are who you say you are, and if Jesus Christ is who you say he is, then you have to prove it to me.'

By shouting like I did, I did not know whether I was crossing a threshold of religious indecency or not. Neither did I care if my yelling at God angered Him. I wanted answers. I needed answers. I knew that I would not be able to sustain this utterly debilitating inability to make any sense of anything for much longer anyway. I was very close to the edge of reason, and the drop that I saw before me was enough to make me tremble with fear.

'Make something of me if you can,' I yelled in the maelstrom of thick volcanic dust that was the cesspit. 'If you are so high and mighty, if you are such a benevolent and kind God, then get me out of this hell and show me that there is something worth living for.'

Nothing happened.

No divine hand came down and plucked me from the hell that was of my own making. Yet in my heart I knew that if there was a God, and if He was the God of the Bible, then He would have heard my cry. It was sincerely sent, it could not have been more sincerely meant, and I hoped and prayed that it would be sincerely received.

Eventually the work started to come to a close. Prisoners were detailed to other duties through injury or because the corporals in charge of the pit decided that they did not need them any more. Paul twisted his back so badly that he was put on light duties in the Pelotón compound. José somehow managed to wangle another posting, and sadly, one friend of mine who I had known from basic training back in Ronda, cracked up in the sun. He started to catch little gecko lizards and eat them, biting their heads off and laughing as the blood dribbled down his chin. The brigada had him beaten and chained to a post in the fort all night on his tiptoes.

That is how it went for others, but every morning my name would be called for the pit, and I was pleased it was. I had decided in my by now sun-crazed mind that my future salvation had something to do with me completing this cesspit, and my determination to see my torment through to the end became almost obsessive.

Even when I smashed up the top of one of my fingers when a large boulder fell on it I refused to be stood down. I pulled the nail out with a pair of pliers so that I could go back to work. I refused to give in, and purposefully pushed myself harder than was necessary. It could not last, I was becoming too tired. I finally passed out when we were wheelbarrowing all the topsoil back on the boulders. I ran instead of walked, ignoring the tightness in my chest and the heaving of my lungs as I ran barrow after barrow back and forth. I heard one of the corporals telling me to slow down, but I refused to listen.

I came back to consciousness in the shade at the back of the kitchen, out of sight of anyone else. Beside me was the corporal with the pipe, sitting on an upturned bin and watching me with curious eyes as he puffed out great plumes of smoke.

I threw up on the ground. My head was pounding and my vision was blurred.

'Why do you do this?' he asked as I sat back wiping my mouth on my sleeve.

'Do what?' I asked.

'Push yourself so hard?'

I shrugged. How could I tell him that I was trying to redeem myself, to salvage some honour from my captivity by making it harder on myself than even they were prepared to?

Just then the skinny corporal turned up with three cold beer bottles.

'Here,' he said, handing me one, along with a cigarette.

At first I thought that it might be a trick, but the pipe smoker nodded when I looked at him for confirmation. I enjoyed that cold beer and the smoke, sitting there in the shade as the two corporals talked about this and that, drinking their own beers, smoking and waiting for me to finish.

'The lorry detail is becoming vacant soon,' the skinny one said as they marched me back to the pit. 'How would you and your friends like to volunteer?'

I said that we would like that very much.

I picked up my wheelbarrow.

'And take it easy,' the pipe smoker said.

I did. Not because I wanted to, but because I couldn't do anything else. I had gone as far as I could, a lot farther than I had imagined, but there was nothing there, no reward, no great revelation, no redemption, just sickness and nausea.

Only a few more days remained before the cesspit was completed, two days ahead of schedule. The brigada would be pleased. I had calmed down a little, but I also knew that I had lost something. I did not quite understand what it was I had lost, but looking back many years later as I can now, I think that I had lost the means to effect any change in my life. Nothing I could do could change anything. I was bereft of options. There was nowhere else for me to go and nothing more I could do. I was as securely pinned as a moth in a display cabinet. All I could do was wait and see if the prayer I had so viciously thrown out into the ether was answered.

Before we finished there was also time for one last drama, one that served to convince me that I had little regard for my life, and shocked me to my core at how enthusiastically I would have welcomed death.

*

A new prisoner had joined our detail, a nervous young lad with thick black-rimmed glasses and an invisible sign around his neck saying "kick me". Without being disrespectful to him it would not be unfair to say that he was not the sharpest tool in the toolbox, and he was so clumsy as to be very dangerous to be around, but none of that was any reason to justify the persecution he suffered at the hands of the guards. He was constantly picked on and made to do stupid things just so they could have a laugh. It was not the full-time corporals who acted in such a way, rather it was two part-timers, one of which was the guard who had pointed a loaded pistol at me on the lorry.

I was not particularly bothered by the fact that he was being bullied, I was sufficiently brutal enough to realise that if they were picking on him then they were leaving me alone. What got my goat was one particular day when the guards persecuted him to the point where he was in tears, then gave him a pistol with which to shoot himself. The guard who had pointed his gun at me on the lorry made a theatrical show of unloading the clip from his Star 9mm semi-automatic and presenting it to the forlorn prisoner at his feet. Without a moment's hesitation the crying prisoner put it in his mouth, barrel first.

'You bloody idiot,' I shouted as I knocked the gun away just before he pulled the trigger, 'there is still one up the spout.'

The gunshot rang out, and a puff of dust next to the guard's foot where the bullet hit justified my action. I felt such a rush of adrenaline and anger I could no more have stopped myself from what I did next as I could have stopped the sun rising.

'You,' I said walking up to the guard and prodding him in the chest, 'are a complete moron. What the hell do you think you are playing at? You nearly killed the poor sod.'

The guard merely looked at me in shock, his mouth hanging open. I was not sure what shocked him most, the gunshot or me prodding and shouting at him.

I went back and picked up the spent casing.

'What are you going to do with that?' the guard asked, having found his voice. 'Give it to me.'

I ignored him and went to sit down. In truth I did not know what I would do with the casing. Show the brigada? Probably not, nobody liked a snitch, but I was so angry I wanted him to sweat.

The guard got angrier, shouting at me to give him the incriminating casing back. I continued to ignore him. I knew what was running through his mind. He had been a sod to most of us prisoners, and now he was a moment away from joining us. There was no way that he would get anything less than Pelotón for what he had done. I knew this and left him to stew.

Stupidly he then reloaded his pistol, cocked it and pointed it at me.

Furious that he had once again pointed his pistol at me, and still full of adrenaline, I jumped up once more and made my way over to him. I did not stop until the barrel of the pistol was up against my chest, aimed directly at my heart. I stared into the by now frightened eyes of the guard just twelve inches from my own.

'That,' I said, 'is the second time you have pointed a loaded pistol at me, and I tell you now that it will be the last. Unless you holster that gun in the next three seconds you will have to kill me, because if you don't pull the trigger I will take it off you and kill you with it myself.'

I dared him to maintain my gaze.

He blinked.

'And if you ever point it at me again, I will kill you, no ifs or buts.'

The other guards shouted at him to lower the pistol; they knew that he would never get out of prison alive if he shot someone in cold blood, and there were enough witnesses to send him away for life. A few of the prisoners also tried to pull me away, but I stood my ground, determined to let him know that I was not frightened of him or his threats. Eventually the guard realised that I was deadly serious, so feigning a laugh that did nothing to hide the nervousness in his voice, he holstered the gun and walked away.

I threw the casing into the hands of the skinny corporal when he got back.

'What happened?' he asked.

'Ask that idiot,' I replied, nodding in the direction of the guard responsible.

Nothing was done. It was decided that the best thing to do was to keep quiet. No one had got hurt, and it would mean a whole heap of trouble for everyone if the brigada ever got to hear about it.

A great sadness engulfed me in the back of the truck on the way back to Pelotón that evening. When I had stood with the gun against my chest earlier, a part of me had wanted him to pull the trigger, so much so that I was almost sorry that he had not. Such a death would have taken the responsibility for it away from me and given it to someone else. It would have been an easy way to die.

Shocked, I asked myself if I had so little respect for my own life as to throw it away in a feat of shallow bravado. The answer that came back disturbed me. Yes! I wanted to die; I did not want to live any more. Although I had come close to suicide so many times before, this time there was a solid resignation to my mindset. Before I had come close to killing myself because I was angry with the world, and because I wanted to hurt those who had hurt me; this time I wanted to die for no other reason than because I was tired and beyond caring.

The only hope I had left was God, and He had been silent since I had challenged Him to prove to me that He existed. So what was there left to do? Where else could I go? I felt like I had been everywhere and done everything I could, and ever so slowly I was reaching the awful conclusion that there was no reason for anything. There was no answer to the riddle of my own existence, because the question had been a foolish one to start off with.

If God cared, He would have done something by now. If He existed at all then why had He not shown himself to me? No Supreme Being I wanted to care about would let someone suffer so much without stepping in to help them. If God did exist then He was a callous and uncaring deity and I wanted nothing to do with Him.

At least that is what I was tempted to believe, but I could not; I was too frightened to believe that no one cared. It is hard to throw away the only lifebelt you had when you were drowning. All I had left to live for was a small spark of hope in a God I had only ever read about, and who seemed as distant from me and as unreachable as the nearest star. Irrespective of the fact that everything I saw around me wanted to convince me that I was being a fool, I clung on to this hope desperately, foolishly.

Little did I know that as I sat there in the back of the truck, wallowing in self-pity, God was already doing something to assuage my sadness. He had heard my challenge, and He was preparing to do the only thing He could do to get through to me. He was preparing to show me something that would break my proud stubborn heart once and for all. In a matter of weeks I was going to come face to face with Jesus Christ himself, and what I was going to see when I did would change everything forever.

CHAPTER ELEVEN

Crucifying the Christ

Hebrews 10:31
It is a dreadful thing to fall into the hands of the living God.

I saw beatings and did not blink; I took beatings and did not blink. I barely had enough compassion to apply to my own aching soul, never mind anyone else's. The brutality of my incarceration had overwhelmed me, and even though I had vowed to remain my own man, by now I was a true product of the system. Physically I felt close to burnout, emotionally I was completely drained and spiritually I was as barren as a desert. It was the lowest I had ever been, before or since.

Life had taken on a weary monotony. By now we had been incarcerated for nearly three months, far longer than the maximum one month normally prescribed. Some of the guards had become friends, and I wondered whether I would ever get out.

Then one day a word started to spread around Pelotón – "indulto!"

I asked what it meant and why the prisoners were getting so excited. José explained.

'There is a big march past coming up,' José said excitedly, 'and it is common at times like this for the colonel to offer an amnesty to all prisoners.'

I laughed.

'Do you honestly expect the colonel to forgive us?'

'Why not?' José replied, his face falling in the presence of my instant pessimism.

'Because the amnesty they are talking about will not apply to us. It will be given to those who are here because they got drunk on duty, or got into a fight on Saturday night, or because there was a button missing on their dress tunic when they turned out for guard. This will not happen to us; we are here for the duration, mate.'

Nevertheless, the preparations for the march past and the ceremony attached to it were put in place, and as they were, the main body of prisoners got themselves overly excited about the prospect of a pardon.

Normally it would have been a service I would have looked forward to. The singing of the Legión hymn as we dipped our flags before the statue of the crucified Christ was always a moving experience. This time though, I would not even see it. Our job was to clean and prepare the parade ground, polish the brass, put out the flags and generally make things presentable. We would then be locked up until the party was over.

Apparently this year, along with a general coming to watch the proceedings, a film crew from the Canary Island TV Station was also going to be there. The professionalism of the Legión was going to be in full view and nothing could be left to chance, everything was going to have to be perfect, and that, of course, meant that we would be working very hard indeed to make it just so.

Standing at ease after lunch one day, a call went out for someone who could paint. I stepped forwards purely on the basis that I had a semblance of talent in this area, and because any job out of the ordinary was a change from the monotony that was by now crippling my mind.

I was handed a large stencil of the Legión emblem. I was also given some paint and paintbrushes, and told to paint this on the whitewashed fresh water tank that sat in the middle of the compound. I set about the job with relish. This was going to be an hour or two of entertainment compared to the usual drudgery of Pelotón. When finished I was justifiably pleased with myself and stood back to admire my handiwork. Just then the brigada made his usually ferocious entrance into the fort.

The brigada's entrance was usually introduced by the cry: 'Sección De Trabajo, El Brigada.'

This was the cue for everyone to panic. It was almost comical as the spirit of the place went from relaxed to fever pitch in the space of a few seconds; even the dogs got caught up in the change of atmosphere and scampered for their kennels. I now realised that the guards were as wary of the brigada as we prisoners, having personally seen more than a few of them catch a blow from his formidable right hand.

I had been given nothing to do in the tumult, so I stood at ease by the freshly painted water tank. Unfortunately for me there was nothing worse in the brigada's eyes than a prisoner standing around doing nothing. He made his way over to me and I braced myself for a beating.

'Aren't you supposed to be doing something?' he asked as he started to take off his white gloves, always a prelude to physical punishment.

'I have just this second finished painting the emblem on the water tank,' I replied, 'and I am awaiting further orders, sir.'

The brigada paused in taking off his gloves and stood back to scrutinise my handiwork. Initially he looked pleased and my heart relaxed. His face then creased into a scowl.

He called me forwards and turned me around to view what I had done.

'Can you tell me what is wrong with this?' he asked.

Frantically I searched the emblem for a mistake.

'No, sir,' I replied, 'I can see nothing wrong.'

He then called over all the corporals.

'Who can tell me what is wrong with this painting?'

There was an awful silence as everyone studied the emblem looking for something, anything wrong with what I had done.

When he realised he had us all over a barrel, theatrically, and with an awful smile, he took off his Chapiri to show us the emblem on it. A sickening realisation then dawned on everyone present, and on me especially; I had painted it the wrong way around. The crossbow and musket were left to right instead of right to left.

Curiously the brigada then smiled.

'Apart from that it is well done,' he said to me.

I was amazed, in ordinary circumstances I would have got a beating.

As the brigada disappeared into his office he asked the guards to keep me to one side for this afternoon because he had a job for me; upon hearing that I decided that I was going to have to stop volunteering.

*

An hour or two later the brigada shouted for me. Coming to attention before him he rattled off an instruction and pointed at the storeroom. Naturally I instantly obeyed his instruction and ran into the store. The unfortunate thing was that I had not understood what the brigada had asked me to fetch. He was difficult to understand at the best of times, his voice was little more than a growl because like most veteran legionarios, the hashish and black tobacco he smoked had decimated his voice box.

After a second or two I realised that the consequence of me appearing out of the store with nothing in my hands was going to result in a beating. I had been lucky to avoid one previously over the episode of the water tank. There was nothing else for it; I was going to have to get it over and done with.

I ran back out of the store and once more came to attention before the brigada.

'I'm sorry, sir,' I said, 'but I didn't quite catch what it was you wanted me to fetch.'

Curiously I thought I saw a trace of sadness flicker across his face. It was one of the few times I had seen anything there except anger. He then mumbled something, pulled off his white gloves and hit me so hard both my feet left the floor. It was a hard hit, and for a second as I lay on the floor I saw stars, but I knew the protocol. I had to be back up on my feet and at attention very quickly or another one would follow. It took me a second or two to steady my legs as I tried to rise, and as I did so I felt a strange sense of calm land upon me - I was having another epiphany.

I realised with sudden clarity that this man can only hurt me physically. He was able to administer pain, but that was it. I then discovered something even stranger; I knew that I was not afraid of him, and more curiously that I actually liked him. He was a hard brutal man, of that there was no doubt, he was capable of great violence, but he was merely doing his job. I knew instinctively that if I had lived his life for the last twenty years I would be no different myself. He was as much a prisoner of the system as I was.

I came to attention again before him, and before I could stop myself I smiled at him.

'So, you think it's funny do you?' he said as he hit me again.

I wanted to explain that I was not laughing at him, I was laughing because I liked him, and because the sun had probably cooked my brain, but I never got the chance. If anything the second blow was harder than the first, and I took a little longer to get back onto my feet, but by this time I was completely beyond caring. He could hit me as much as he wanted, but I knew in my heart that I had beaten him and the system. I was no longer afraid of him or anything else they could throw at me. What hurt most was having no reason to live; everything else was immaterial in the face of this loss.

When you came to attention before a superior officer, etiquette dictated that you come close, but not too close. You have to show bravery and a confidence that indicated you were willing to accept any order given, but you were not supposed to get so close as to show disrespect. Normally I would not have, but this time was different, as I came back to attention I pushed myself farther into his face than was normally accepted, and said something so completely and utterly stupid as to make me wonder whether I was a complete lunatic.

'Gracias, mi brigada, otra, por favor.'

There was an audible gasp from everyone present. As far as they were concerned I had just signed my own death warrant. I had just thanked the brigada for hitting me and asked him for another one.

Sadness tinged with confused bewilderment flickered across the brigada's face.

'What did you say?' he asked.

'I said thank you, sir, and could I have another one please,' I replied, bracing myself for the beating of a lifetime.

What happened in the next few seconds was completely unexpected. The bewilderment left, and slowly a smile crept up onto the brigada's face. It was as wary as a bat in daylight, but it came out nevertheless. He then began to laugh, and instead of a beating me he put his arm over my shoulders and led me into the store. Behind me I could almost feel the stunned silence as the rest of the Pelotón watched this curious going on.

'All I wanted you to get was some paint and paintbrushes, you idiot,' he said, still smiling.

Apparently there were some plaques around the parade ground that needed a fresh coat of paint, and the brigada had decided that I was the one to do it. Something even stranger happened then. Instead of getting one of the guards to take me, he took me himself. It was a very strange occurrence. I had never seen it happen before, and by the look on the other guards' and prisoners' faces as he led me out of the compound, neither had anyone else.

It was a quiet and surreal time with the brigada. He stood guard behind me as I painted, explaining to me in his gruff voice which regiments the plaques belonged to and their history. He was very knowledgeable about Legión history and obviously loved his regiment.

Naturally I was incredibly nervous in the face of this unexpected civility, and because of this on one plaque I missed a black line. Instead of whacking me around the head, the brigada took the paintbrush out of my hand, pushed me to one side and started to paint it himself. I was then in the curious situation of standing behind the brigada watching him work. I wondered what strange parallel universe I had fallen into.

A second or two later a cry went up behind me. I came to attention when I saw who it was that hailed us. It was the colonel on the other side of the parade ground. The brigada cursed as he recognised the voice, put the paintbrush back into my hand and ran over to report.

Out of the corner of my eye I watched nervously as the colonel used his swagger stick to prod the brigada a few times, obviously making a determined point about something. I could only assume that the colonel had recognised me as one of the deserters and was wondering why I was watching the brigada do my job, or why I was on such light duties. After a minute or two the brigada saluted and ran back to where I was still stood to attention.

The by now out-of-breath and flush-faced brigada indicated that I was to continue with my painting. He then proceeded to tell me exactly what he thought of the colonel and the whole officer class. The whole invective was full of unadorned expletives and derogatory comments. A few seconds later, as he left the parade ground, the colonel shouted out something I did not quite hear in the brigada's direction, I cannot print the brigada's mumbled reply.

After that he was silent for a while, and I slowly started to breathe again.

'You're to be court-martialled,' he said after a while.

'I had expected that, sir,' I replied, not lifting my eyes from my painting.

'It would not have happened in my day,' he said. 'Do you know how many years I spent as a prisoner in Pelotón during my first five years as a legionario?'

'I have no idea, sir,' I replied.

'Two,' he said.

I dared a glance up at him, and was surprised to see a strange pride in his eyes.

'It took them five years to break me in, and I am glad they did. I was a no good thief and layabout, and heading for prison before I joined the Legión. Now I am a brigada,' he said proudly.

I was mystified as to why he was telling me all this.

'You have done well so far,' he said, 'and I am certain that if given a second chance you would not make the same mistake, would you?'

'No, sir,' I replied, 'I wish to God I could turn the clock back and start again. I like it here; I wanted to make the Legión my home.'

'That's what I thought,' the brigada replied, 'and it's exactly what the modern Legión doesn't understand. Sometimes the best legionarios are the ones you have to break in. It can't expect to be the hardest unit in the Spanish Army if it doesn't give the men it needs a second chance every now and then.'

He said no more after that, and for the next hour as I finished my painting I was left with mixed feelings. I felt a great sadness upon confirmation of the fact that I was to be court-martialled, but also a silent joy that one of the hardest men ever to put on a Legión uniform had given me his coded encouragement.

Back at the fort I told Paul and José that we were to be court-martialled. They both smiled and looked pleased.

'Thank God for that,' Paul said, 'did he say when?'

I shook my head.

*

That night, as the cell door was locked behind me, I lay on my thin yellow mattress and cursed my fate and the fact that I had once again brought myself to ignominy. What was there for me now? Where else could I go? Disaster and failure had plagued my footsteps my whole life, and the worst part of knowing this was that there was no one else to blame for my predicament except myself.

It was true that I had gained a small glimmer of satisfaction by being acknowledged by the brigada, but at what cost, and to what purpose? In the great scheme of things would this change me or my outlook on life? Had I found something of substance I could build my life upon? Probably not; my determination to squeeze some honour out of my predicament had achieved nothing of any eternal consequence. Inside I felt as empty as ever. In fact, I probably felt worse, knowing for certain as I did now that I would have made a good soldier if it had not been for José and Paul's madcap scheme to desert.

Stripped bare emotionally as I was that night, I asked God once again to intervene in my life. There was no anger in my prayer this time, no bitterness about the state I was in, just silent tears in the darkness, and a grim determination to hang on to some semblance of hope in a world that seemed to have robbed me of it.

What I did not know as I lay there feeling sorry for myself in the dark and cloying prison cell was that the following day was to be the single most important day in my life up until then.

*

The following morning started the same as any other. The door burst open at five, and we were lined up ready for the day's instructions. With a squad of others I wandered the camp with my bucket and brush until after breakfast when, instead of being sent out on the lorry as normal, a few of us, myself and José included, were picked for a special duty. We did not know what it was until we were halted in front of the officers' chapel.

Led inside I gazed reverentially upon the statue given the most prominent position in the chapel. It was a life-sized model of Jesus in all His suffering on the cross, the same one that had pride of place on the cenotaph for ceremonial days like tomorrow, and I had never been as close to it as I was then. It was a humbling experience, and curiously painful to see the crown of thorns on His head and the blood running from the wound in His side, even though I knew that it was only red paint.

'We've got to get the statue out of here and up onto the cross,' our guard coldly stated.

Once outside we got the figure up onto our shoulders. Standing at the front as I was, I suddenly got the sensation of all the weight being given to me. Behind I heard José whispering to the other two prisoners.

'Leave him,' he said, 'he will carry it all by himself if we let him. He's into all this religious stuff.'

José had always found my Christianity - or rather my attempts at it - something to mock. I could have challenged him as the weight bit into my shoulders, but I didn't. Instead I felt a curious desire to carry the statue all by myself, remembering how a man called Simon of Cyrene was picked out of the crowd by the Roman soldiers crucifying Jesus, and forced to carry the cross for Him.

José and the others then started whispering about their chances of an "indulto" again.

'What was it that Jesus said when he was on the cross, Mark?' José asked as we carried the cross from the chapel and across the parade ground towards the cenotaph.

Carrying the cross had started a whirlpool of emotions in my heart, and I was only just able to repeat the words I remembered.

'He said, "Father forgive them for they know not what they do".'

A set of ladders was put up against the pillar, and I was ordered to climb them. I had been given the dubious honour of placing the crucified Christ in the metal cradle that would support Him throughout the coming day's celebrations. It was there under that hot summer sun that my heart was broken forever.

There was only room for one on the ladder, and as I heaved the full weight of the statue upwards using a rope passed up to me tied around the Christ, I realised exactly what it was that I was doing. It seemed to me in my heightened state of emotion that I had been transported back two thousand years, and I was now taking part in the crucifixion ceremony all over again. The question that came to me as I imagined the sights and sounds of ancient Jerusalem was this: in the story of the passion, what part would I have best been suited to playing?

Where was I when Jesus was crucified?

I quickly realised that I was no Simon of Cyrene at the crucifixion. I was no innocent bystander in the crowd watching the day's events unfold only to be dragged into it through no fault of my own, and I certainly was not a disciple, rather the part that suited me best was playing one of the soldiers who actually nailed Him to the cross.

I was no stranger to history; I knew just how vicious the men of the Roman Legions had been. They were ferocious warriors who would have taken part in such an act without batting an eyelid. Men who would beat one of their own comrades to death for falling asleep on guard, or for showing cowardice in the face of the enemy, would not consider crucifying a Jew an arduous task.

Palestine was regarded by the rank and file as one of the worst postings in the whole Roman Empire. They were hated by the Jews, who resented the Roman occupation in spite of the peace it brought to their otherwise troubled land. The Romans hated the Jews in return, despising their independent spirit and monotheistic religion, so far removed from their own belief system.

In history the soldiers at the cross are vilified as uncaring men, who had their sport at Christ's expense before they nailed Him to His cross and cast lots for His clothes. Yet in what way would I have been any different? The answer that came back brought me close to desperation. It was a revelation that cut me to the very core of my being, yet it was one that I was completely unable to deny, because given the same circumstances I would have done exactly the same thing myself.

The Roman soldiers knew what it was to survive in an atmosphere of brutal discipline, and I also knew something about that. I had become a product of a system of violence that was supposed to turn me into a soldier capable of killing without emotion, as they had themselves. They were soldiers who were expected to obey their orders irrespective of their own individual conscience, and I could also say that I knew something about that. I was even speaking Spanish, which has its roots in Latin.

My pride would like to think that I would have conducted myself differently from the other soldiers at Golgotha, but my experiences over the last few months had convinced me that I would not. In my heart I knew that if given the same circumstances as those Romans, I would have personally plaited the crown of thorns and then pushed it hard down onto His head. Shamefacedly I also knew that if handed the whip I would have laid into Him with as much determination as did the original man to beat Him. With sickening sadness I knew that if I had been ordered to, I would have even hammered in the nails.

God help me, but it was as if I had been there in person doing it.

My words here cannot truly convey the pain of such a revelation. It was the purest form of shame I have ever known. I was exposed to myself and the world as a complete fraud. I was no Christian at all. In fact, as I pulled Jesus Christ up to His cross, I knew that I was as far from God as it was possible to be. I was not a good man in any way, shape or form. My attempts at life had finally proved to me that I was nothing more than a wastrel. Most of all though, I was ashamed of myself because I had dared to ask this God to help me; I had dared to believe that He might listen to a loser like me. It seemed ridiculous to me as I hauled up the Christ to his position, that I had asked a man for help whom I was as capable of killing with the same reckless abandon as those who did at Golgotha all those years ago.

I knew that I deserved nothing from this man, neither could I expect anything in answer to my prayers, so why, as I lifted Him up by his armpits to drop Him into his cradle, did tears start to stream down my face, and from where did I manage to summon up the courage to speak to Him again?

Maybe it was because I knew then with a conviction born of a certainty that has never left me since, that this man was the Son of God. No man could have died the way He did. Led like a lamb to the slaughter, forgiving the men who nailed Him to the cross and even offering salvation to the thief crucified beside Him. That is not how normal men die. I read later in the Bible how the centurion in charge of the crucifixion was moved to comment that "surely this man was the Son of God", and I could do no other. Such a death was beyond the capacity of a normal man. He could only have been whom He said He was, and it was this revelation alone that prompted me to speak.

'You asked God to forgive those men who crucified you all those years ago,' I said, gazing into the sad and lifeless eyes of the statue, as tears now fell unbidden down my cheeks, much to the amusement of José and his friends below me, 'and now I ask you to please forgive me.'

I expected no reply to my prayer. He had not answered me before, but I needed Him to know that I felt wretched. Finally I understood what it was to acknowledge my sin. I had run away from my Bible earlier because I did not want to understand why or how I was a sinner, preferring my ignorance to enlightenment. Now I was powerless to refuse the logic of the notion that I was a sinner, and that I desperately needed a saviour.

Then I heard Him... and I heard Him with a clarity that I can still feel in that part of me that guards the memory of His voice with a trembling fear and devotion, and what He said shook me then, and shakes me still.

Mark, I love you, and I forgive you.

The lips of the statue did not move, nor did I imagine that the voice came from the statue itself, even though it was the focal point of my devotion. The words came directly from Heaven, and they were unequivocally the words of God, and I will attest to them being so until the day I die.

I do not know what is literally meant by the "audible voice of God", but I can explain my experience in no other way. What was said to me was not spoken into my ear the way normal words are, but rather they were spoken directly into my soul, reaching into that deepest and most sacred part of me; that part of every human being that only God Himself truly has access to, the only place in a man from which He can order change.

Someone at my church on the Alpha Course came to me the other week and asked me how it is you know when God is speaking to you. I told them that you know it is the Lord when what He says to you is beyond your own intelligence to conjure. It is God when what is said is so profound and deep as to leave you troubled, blessed and breathless.

It is true that God speaks to us in many ways: by dreams, visions, wisdom and prophesy. So often when we say or hear such things, they have first been filtered down so much by our own imagination as to render what is said almost lifeless in content. I confess to having heard and spoken many such words myself since my salvation, yet nothing has ever succeeded in moving me so much as to hear my own Lord God forgive me that hot summer day at the cenotaph of the Third Tercio.

Something snapped inside me upon receipt of the words, and this is not merely a metaphor. I heard and felt something break. It was almost the same sound a lollipop stick makes when a child snaps it in two, and I have often wondered what such a noise was. My only explanation is that this was the moment my spirit finally broke.

So long I had been fighting. So long I seemed to have been resisting the world and the sadness it wanted to heap upon me, that in the end I was unable to resist the weight of such love as I heard that fateful day. I had vowed that no man would break me, how wrong I had been to utter such proud words. Christ the man had shattered me into small pieces, and my spirit was forever broken in the face of such grace. Whose would not be? Where beatings and rejection had failed to work, a few simple words spoken in pure and undying love had succeeded.

God had answered the challenge I had thrown out at Him as I dug the cesspit. He had waited and moved the chess pieces of my life until He had me exactly where He wanted me. He had worked upon me with the skill born of a master craftsman. He knew that a stubborn heart like mine would only believe if I saw with my own eyes who and what He was. Now I had seen, and now I was a believer, and I knew that I had been yoked to a burden of such gracious loving insight as to make me completely unable to deny the fact that Jesus Christ was, and still is, the Son of the Almighty God.

'You are the Christ,' I answered in reply to the forgiveness offered. 'You truly are the Son of God, and I pledge myself to you now. I vow to follow you all the days of my life.'

As I spoke the words I knew that this was no transient commitment. This was no New Year's Resolution waiting to be flung away like an old sweet wrapper the following day. My heart had been won by a man who deserved everything I could offer, and I was determined to give it to Him. Never would I need to search again for the truth. Never would I need to seek out which direction my life would take. I had found the reason for living, the reason for my existence - it was to follow the Christ.

At last, at long last, I had found the adventure my soul had been craving. The thing I had been seeking was here before me now. I was to become a disciple of Jesus Christ, and I would remain so until the day I died. I had found the way, the truth and the life. Nothing was clearer, nothing was more obvious, and as I sit here in my office at home many years later writing this, the events of that day move me still, and I commit myself anew to my vow, thanking God that He has seen fit to supply the grace I have needed each and every day in order to keep me true to my word.

CHAPTER TWELVE

El Castillo De San Francisco Del Risco

John 3: 5-6
Jesus answered, 'I tell you the truth, no one can enter the kingdom of God unless he is born of water and the Spirit. Flesh gives birth to flesh, but the Spirit gives birth to spirit.'
You should not be surprised at my saying, 'You must be born again.'

Previous to my meeting with Christ at the cross, I had been uninspired as to what direction my life should be taking. I had no dreams or desire beyond the court martial and my expulsion from the Legión. Neither had I any inclination as to what might become of me. Now everything had changed. I was charged with a phenomenal desire to know more about Jesus. Where I went or what I did after the Legión was immaterial in the face of this passion. I had been filled with a yearning I could barely contain. This Jesus was the future on which I was going to build the rest of my life, and I wanted to know who He was, and what He had done and said in its entirety.

Unfortunately, being a prisoner meant that I was not allowed any reading material, not even the Bible, and how I cursed myself for a fool for not having read more of the Good News version my mother had sent me, the one that was now sat at the bottom of my locker gathering dust. It was all there, the whole story, a mere twenty yards from the fort. All I had to help me along until I could get my hands on it were the few tangled memories I could conjure from films I had seen, religious education classes at school, and the bits of the Bible I had read previously that had not slipped through my memory.

It is amazing though what the mind can remember when you are desperate, what can be squeezed from the dark recesses of the memory when you concentrate like you never have before. What I was able to recollect fed me until I could get to the fountain of life that I was sure lay between the covers of my Bible.

What struck me was how different everything was now, especially how different Christianity appeared now that I had seen the founder of the movement face to face. Gone was my previous confusion as to how Christianity was supposed to interact with my life, or the idea that the Christianity of the established Church was irrelevant to me. Jesus Christ had never seemed more relevant. I was still confused as to why the Church meandered around the subject in the way it did. Why it had built up such a theological smoke screen around what appeared to be a plain and simple truth. However, who was I to argue with the Church? All I wanted to do was to get my hands on the Bible in my locker and read it: every day without it was agony. Yet I was going to have to wait another two months before I was able to study it.

Pelotón had not finished with me yet.

*

Life continued much as it always had in prison. Myself, José and Paul were now regulars on the lorry, and we enjoyed the perks of the position. Such was our standing that we were even asked by the guards who it was we wanted to be the fourth member of the crew when the position became vacant.

It is a strange thing to come to terms with the violence that was our everyday life, but it all seemed so normal after a while. I barely blinked even when the brigada got six weeks of house arrest for bursting the eardrums of a guard who had let his troop of prisoners sit down and have a smoke. Even though I liked the guard in question, a large Asturian who had joined the Legión rather than go down the coal mines of his Northern Spanish home, as would have been his fate otherwise. I was glad at the news; it meant that for the rest of my tenure the discipline in the fort was able to wind itself down to an acceptable level without the fear of the brigada stalking us.

As inured as I was to the sometimes appalling levels of violence I saw, even I was shocked by some things that happened in the crazy world that was Pelotón.

One evening, a few hours after lights out, we were woken suddenly by the cell door being opened. Still in a deep sleep we struggled to get ourselves ready. Outside in the compound we heard loud voices and angry shouts. Something was obviously very wrong.

To our surprise a lieutenant stepped through the doorway. After the initial shock of the smell that set him back a couple of steps, he told us not to bother getting dressed, all he wanted was a headcount. When this had been done the door was closed as we, full of curiosity, gathered around the window to see what was going on outside.

'What's happening?' I asked José who was next to me.

'It seems like someone has told the duty officer of the guard that Corporal Keitas is raping one of the prisoners,' he replied quite nonchalantly.

I looked at him incredulously.

I then remembered that a few weeks ago José had pointed out one of the newest prisoners. He was a quiet and portly lad with sad eyes, who had been put on domestic duty by Keitas as soon as he had arrived. Domestic duty was a particularly loathsome job, albeit light work. It meant that you cleaned and cooked for the permanent guards, acting no better than a skivvy to them. He told me that this particular prisoner was having sex with Keitas. I disbelieved him, as I distrusted just about everything I heard from José.

Keitas was a permanent lance-corporal and a particularly nasty specimen. Nearly all the other guards I found I could manipulate in some way or other, all except Keitas. He was seemingly impenetrable, and around him I kept my head down and did exactly what I was told at all times. He laughed when I got dizzy from fatigue because I had a bad case of the runs and was not retaining my fluids and was brought back into the fort by two other prisoners.

'What's the matter,' he said, 'can you see the sun and the stars spinning?'

I was too groggy to reply, so he hit me.

'Here,' he said as he punched and kicked me all around the yard, 'let's see if you can see any more heavenly bodies spinning across the sky.'

It was a painful reminder of the fact that Keitas was a man of little sympathy and a cruel temperament.

'Keitas is gay?' I asked.

José laughed.

'Man,' he said, 'sometimes I wonder what planet you are on. Of course he is gay, everyone knows that.'

Still unable to believe the news I turned back to watch the proceedings outside our cell window.

The lieutenant had by now deduced that there was one prisoner missing from the roll call, and he seemed to know exactly where to find him. Marching over to Keitas's room he banged on the door and demanded entry. At first there was no reply from inside.

'Keitas is for it now,' everyone whispered, and undisguised glee ran through the whole of us as we prepared to watch him get his comeuppance.

After more banging and further demands at entry by the lieutenant, Keitas's voice was heard on the other side of the door.

'This prisoner is here to sleep only,' he shouted.

Even I could hear the fear in his voice. Any form of homosexual activity was a court martial offence, and was particularly frowned upon by a force that modelled itself as a morally principled Christian Army.

When the door finally opened, the prisoner and Keitas stepped out, confirming what José had said all along. The lieutenant went completely berserk, and we were given the pleasure of watching him batter the hapless guard all over the compound. When Keitas was finally marched away under guard, we settled down on our mattresses and discussed what would happen to him.

'He could end up in here with us,' someone said, and there was a general murmur from everyone present that this would be no bad thing.

He had hurt many of those present, and I shuddered inwardly at the thought of what would happen to him when the door slammed shut on his first night alone with us. I doubted whether he would make it out alive.

'No,' someone else said, 'they will pension him off to avoid a scandal.'

We never saw Keitas again, and I never did find out what happened to him or whether he was guilty of rape, but I was glad to see him go.

Not every incident was quite so traumatic. Sometimes we were able to laugh at the strange things that happened in our crazy world.

On one occasion, not long after Keitas had been arrested, we were greeted by a very strange sight, one that had us in gales of laughter. This incident also happened after we had been locked up for the night, as once again we awoke to angry shouts in the yard. Looking out of the window we could not quite believe the sight that met our eyes.

There in the yard, surrounded by angry guards, was a massive legionario, well over six feet tall, but what made the sight so incongruous was that he was dressed in a nun's habit. From what we could gather from the guards screaming at him, he had dressed himself like this and attempted to board the ferry at Corralejo, seemingly under the noses of the military police out looking for him. He might even have got away with it if he had been of slight build, who would want to arrest a nun? But this guy was as wide as he was tall, and built like a boxer.

'Look,' one of the howling prisoners shouted with delight, 'his habit doesn't even reach the floor.'

Sure enough his black habit was at least five inches too short, and exposed his hairy calves above his dress uniform shoes. It was one of the funniest things I had ever seen in my life, and like all the others I laughed until I cried, even as he got a beating from the guards, who by now were trying to staunch their own sniggers. When he was finally thrown in with us we gave him a cheer and clapped him on the back. It was an audacious attempt at escape, and worthy of our respect.

Such spectacles proved to be only short interludes in what was becoming an interminable time for the three of us. Pelotón was teaching us nothing new. We had learnt all we could from the regime. The work section was only supposed to be a "short sharp shock", and even to the guards it was as if we had outstayed our welcome. It did not help them that by now we knew every trick in the book, and were adept at using them.

I wish I could say that from the moment I committed myself to Jesus I became a model disciple, but I cannot. In my defence, I was confused about what had happened, and in spite of my determination to now follow Jesus, I was slightly scared about committing myself to something that I would end up blowing again. Yet I can also say that something had definitely changed. My conscience, for one, had decided to intervene in most aspects of my life, and the sinful things I had previously partaken of without a qualm, now started to taste bitter in my stomach.

What had actually happened to me? Was it normal? Was I mad? I was not sure about anything much. Something had changed in me, but something inside also told me that there was more to what had been started. I felt as though I had been half-painted, as if the artist had left me in the middle of my portrait to take a break and had not come back. It was a curious feeling to be left suspended as I was, and it only heightened my desire to know more. With a daily prolonged desperation I knew that there was only one thing that would help me, and how I longed to read my Bible. I felt like a man dying of thirst held back just inches from the cool water of the desert oasis.

*

The end of our Pelotón punishment came unexpectedly one Sunday. We were sweeping the floor of the compound with the reed brushes the way we had been forced to sweep the parade ground during our first few days of prison, and once again my back was threatening to give out on me. As was normal by this time I was praying and asking God to help me get through the day, when all of a sudden Paul, José and I were called from the ranks.

We were stood at ease by the office and given a cigarette each as one by one the guards came up and shook our hands.

'You're to be transferred to the main military prison on Gran Canaria,' one of the corporals told us, 'there you will be sentenced.'

Our joy at hearing the news was tempered only by the thought of what our sentence would be, and whether they would take our time in Pelotón into account; a total of five back-breaking months.

The corporal with the pipe then came forwards.

'We are to take you to your company where you will collect your kitbags. From there you will spend the night in the cells at the north gate in the care of the military police. Monday or Tuesday morning you will be taken to Gran Canaria.'

One by one we were then called into the office to sign a couple of papers. My joy at hearing that I was at last going to get my hands on my Bible was enormous, far outweighing any joy I had at seeing the back of Pelotón.

Inside the office the pipe-smoking corporal looked me deep in the eyes after I had signed the papers.

'I have never seen that before,' he said.

'Not seen what?' I asked.

'Prisoners being sent on their way with a cigarette and a handshake,' he replied.

I wanted to say that it was difficult not to become friends with the men who guard you when you are in such close proximity for so long. It was just over five months since we had first put on the blue boiler suit, and that was the longest sentence I or anyone else had heard of in many years. However, I remained silent, not sure where the conversation was going.

'It is a shame,' he said to me, 'you would have made a fine legionario, maybe even a sergeant or brigada in time.'

It was hard not to be moved by what he said, as once again I felt relief that at least my decision to work hard and suffer my punishment honourably had gone some way to convincing the men who guarded me that I was not a complete waste of space.

'Thank you,' I said. 'Thank you very much.'

I can remember little about our departure for Gran Canaria and the prison there, which I learned was called "El Castillo De San Francisco Del Risco". I cannot even remember whether we flew or went by boat. My whole time was spent reading my Bible; that I can remember, but my joy was short-lived as once again my belongings were taken from me when we arrived at the prison.

'It is just for a short while,' a young and smiling Legión Brigada told us as he took away our kitbags, 'until your paperwork has been processed and you are admitted into the main prison population.'

For two days we were housed in a cell reminiscent of something out of the Middle Ages. The door was an old-fashioned metal bar affair and the walls were smooth rock hewn from the mountain itself. I was to learn later that the castle had once been attacked by that scourge of the Spanish, Sir Francis Drake, but had successfully held out against him.

Eventually we were moved into the main prison population of approximately eighty inmates and allocated our cells. The cells were clean if rudimentary. In each cell there were usually four, three-tier bunks, a locker each with no key, and a toilet. We also had a small television and thankfully the food was good. Compared to Pelotón it was the Dorchester. There were two sides to the prison; one for those awaiting sentencing, and one for those who had been. We were billeted in the former.

For the first couple of weeks I barely moved off my bunk except to eat or go to the toilet. I was completely engrossed in my Bible. I read it from beginning to end before deciding that the only parts that interested me were what Jesus said and did, whereupon I worked my way methodically through the Gospels.

Initially I was bunked with Paul and José, but I was to learn something that was to seriously damage our relationship. It all came about because I was so engrossed in my reading and all things "Jesus", as to render me almost too religious to be around. Much to the annoyance of Paul, who was completely disinterested in religion, merely wanting someone to be his mate who was not always banging on about God. I tried to keep my conversation on other things, but I was unable to.

One day Paul suggested that we swap letters from home. I agreed, but as I started reading Paul's letter I realised something quite terrible. There was no mention whatsoever of the injuries his mum was supposed to have suffered in the after-effects of the car bomb - the whole reason I had been suckered into the desertion plan in the first place. When I confronted Paul about this, he confessed that there never had been a bomb. He told me that it was a lie José had come up with to win me over to their crazy plan.

At first I was angry and drew away from Paul and José, blaming them for my predicament, but the more I thought about it the more I realised that I should not have believed them in the first place. Although worldly-wise in so many ways, I could be as gullible and naive as a child in others. Injured by a car bomb? Even as I thought about it, it flew in the face of reason. I calmed down when I realised that I had been as guilty as they were for believing such a cock and bull story. Besides, there was nothing I could do about it now anyway. I was where I was because I had been a fool, and nothing on earth could ever change that. Getting too angry was nothing more than a distraction. I had my Bible to read and, God willing, an adventure to plan!

One thing did spring up in the light of this new evidence though. I resolved that if the opportunity arose and I could go back to my company on Fuerteventura, I would tell them what Paul and José had done, how they had lied, and I would attempt to clear my name. This I decided would be the righteous thing to do. Only later would this decision come back to haunt me in a completely unexpected way.

My falling out with Paul and José precipitated a change of cells for them, as they found new mates in a prison population composed of the dregs and misfits of every army unit based in the Canaries. I remained where I was in a cell with some reasonably nice lads who generally left me to my own devices. Paul unfortunately got himself involved in the main mafia who ran the prison's extortion and blackmail syndicate, and José decided to pair up with a guy who styled himself as one of the wannabe main drug dealers in the prison.

I have many regrets as to my conduct during my incarceration; and drugs always loom large as one of them. Locked up in a cell no bigger in size than the normal household living room with eleven other guys, it is not easy to get away and spend some quality time on your own. I often woke up resolving to say no to the next joint that was passed around, only to find myself as high as a kite the same evening clapping along as one of the other prisoners sang a mournful flamenco song.

The other problem was that they all knew that I was on a foreigner's wage, three times more than anyone else in the prison apart from Paul, and as far as they were concerned that meant more drugs for everyone who could get alongside me. Something I was never allowed to forget was every toke I had taken on someone else's joint, especially when they knew I had money in my pocket. In prison, nothing was free or without its attached political repercussions.

It was usually when we had been locked up for the night that we smoked the dope, with a few tame guards actually doing the ferrying of drugs between cells. During the day we were left to our own devices, and I spent most of my time trying to find a quiet corner alone so I could read my Bible in peace. I gradually became enamoured with it. The more I read about Jesus Christ and the type of life He led, the more I grew angry with the Church for misrepresenting Him.

Jesus was a revolutionary; a man of deep principles and an unswerving commitment to the justness of His cause. The Church seemed to have tamed Him somehow, presenting Him as a tame lion, when in fact He was completely wild. The more I read, the more I became convinced that I had made the correct decision in committing myself to Him at the cross. He had power and an obviously electrifying personality. How else could He command men to follow Him, and they get up and leave everything behind there and then?

As to His divinity, as far as I was concerned it was beyond doubt. I had seen enough evidence of His Godhead at the cross, and you only had to read the Sermon on the Mount or hear His words of comfort to the sick and hurting to know that you were in the presence of God. His eloquence was beyond being inspiring or merely articulate. It was awesome. Sometimes, somewhere on the planet, at random points in history, someone says or writes something beautiful; and the power of the beauty in the words echoes for centuries to come. Jesus went way beyond that. Not only did it seem that He could not open His mouth without saying something that would rock human civilisation forever, but His whole demeanour backed up His words so completely as to leave Him beyond criticism or reproach. He lived and died as beautifully as He spoke. He was the real deal - the perfect man.

More than anything else during this time, I put great store in His words because they were the only link I had to Him as an individual. It was true that I had to trust that His words had been transcribed correctly by those writing or translating the Gospels, but such beauty once heard could never be forgotten. It was inconceivable to me that the disciples or anyone else could have made this up, so I believed that what I was reading was as from the very lips of Christ Himself.

All the while I read an ache grew within me. You ladies will have to forgive me this metaphor, but it was like I was waiting to give birth. Every day my anticipation that something dramatic was about to happen increased, filling me with a hope I was barely able to contain. Something was waiting for me, something more than I had experienced at the cross, and the key to it was hidden in the words I was now reading.

Feverishly I devoured the parables. Over and over again I read the words spoken by Jesus, which I had underlined in red. One night, after lights out, angry that I was unable to read any more, I prayed.

'Whatever it is you want me to know then you are going to have to help me find it.'

A day or two later I alighted upon the Parable of the Lost Son in the Gospel of Luke, Chapter 15, a parable I had previously read with the old eye of someone who had been weaned on the story since childbirth. What child of the Christian West does not learn how the youngest son asks his father for his share of the inheritance early, only to squander it in a foreign land? It is a part of the folklore of our country and every other Christian land since the Bible was first put together.

Nevertheless, this was the parable that gripped my heart like a vice. The key to the unlocking of my eternal soul was in this simple story, of that I became increasingly certain. I could not put it down. I read it and tried to move on many times, only to be drawn back to it like a moth to the candle. I must have read it a hundred times, and every time I did my heart felt the pressure of eternity squeezing it with an expectation beyond words.

The drug supply abruptly stopped. A clampdown had been imposed after one of the guards was found with hashish on him that he had bought on the outside for an inmate. For over a week there were no drugs in the prison, and for the first time in many months my head cleared.

I believe now that this was what God had been waiting for; because now it happened. The light of reason that touches all those who ask God to reveal Himself to them from the pages of His word touched me, and the Parable of the Lost Son came to life in a way that I still tremble about when I think of it.

I already knew that the son was a symbol of all mankind, a representation of humanity going our own way and squandering our inheritance. I knew that now we ate the slops of the pigs where we could have been feasting at the table of the father; that was obvious. You only had to look at the world around you to know that it was so. A hidden gem in the story I had previously missed only now began to gleam. I read how the son was so humiliated by his fall from grace that he reasoned that even the slaves in his father's household were treated better than he was. He then decided to go back home - and here my heart started to shudder with excitement at what I read – because he was going to ask his father to accept him back, not as a son, rather as a slave.

What could have prompted a man to believe that he would not be welcome in his own father's house, but true shame? This son had reached a place that I understood completely. He had blown it as I had, and now all he wanted was to be allowed to go back home, and he did not care as to the position he would take when he got back. He had no pride left to cling to, no self-respect or honour with which to bolster himself. In looking after the pigs, he was as low as he could possibly go.

I fell into the story and felt the pain of this young man. I empathised with him completely. I too had made a shipwreck of my life, and I had nowhere else to go but back to my Father in Heaven. I put the Bible down and told God that when I was able to get out of this prison I would seek Him out, I would do whatever it took to find Him. I would even become a monk if He thought it necessary.

Only when I picked the Bible back up did the light come on in my understanding, for I read that as the son made his way back home the father saw him a "long way off and ran to meet him".

'But surely,' I reasoned to myself, 'if that is me going home, then that is the father running to meet me too!'

I turned my face to the bars on the window, closed my eyes and held out my hands to Heaven. I asked God to forgive me and accept me back into His family. Instinctively, I now knew that I did not have to go anywhere, because the Father had seen me coming a long way off and was now running to meet me.

There and then, free from all the restraint my sin had previously imposed upon Him, the Spirit of God was able to administer the miracle of new birth. In a microsecond I was washed clean of my sins and accepted into the family of God. I knew a peace beyond words, and the burden of life that I had carried with me from my earliest memories slipped off me and crawled away to die in the darkness where it belonged.

In the parable, the son has a robe put on his back by his father, a ring on his finger and shoes on his feet. His father covers his son's shame with the garments of love and sonship - so it was for me. My embittered and war-weary soul had finally come home, and God was clothing me with the garments of praise and peace.

I was now a free man.

Nothing has ever been the same. I was a new man as only the gift of spiritual new birth can bring about. God had reached into my soul and lit up that which had previously been in darkness. Oh, the joy of that moment! It was indescribable, and I was rendered speechless by the power of it.

However, there was more to come!

CHAPTER THIRTEEN

Baptised in the Shower

Acts 2: 1-4
When the day of Pentecost came they were all together in one place.
Suddenly a sound like the blowing of a violent wind came from heaven
and filled the whole house where they were sitting.
They saw what seemed to be tongues of fire that separated and came to
rest on each of them.
All of them were filled with the Holy Spirit and began to speak in other
tongues as the Spirit enabled them.

If being born again was all God had for me I would have been satisfied. All my burdens and cares had been removed from me in an instant, and a joy of life had taken the place of my previous chronic melancholia. Life was now filled with endless possibilities, and in spite of my circumstances I was certain that my future looked rosy.

Once again though, I became convinced that there was more. I read Acts, and how the apostles had been turned from quivering men full of fear into bold speakers of God's word upon receipt of the Holy Spirit, so I decided that I wanted that too. I did not know then that many Christian denominations claim that the Baptism of the Holy Spirit was a one-time act in order to kick-start the Church. I did not care as to whether or not I was upsetting anybody's sensibilities or theological convictions. All I cared about was getting everything from God that He was prepared to give me.

You might want to call it greed. You might even want to call it arrogance of a colossal nature. I did not care. I saw men getting something awesome and I also wanted it, so I asked God for the gift of the Holy Spirit, but first I decided that I needed to be baptised. Not baptised as I had been by the sprinkling of a few drops of water on my head as an infant, but the baptism of full immersion as demonstrated by Jesus Himself. As far as I was concerned, if Jesus decided that getting baptised was important in order for Him to fulfil all righteousness, then who was I do decide that baptism by full immersion was not important? I was beyond deciding what to take and what to refuse, I wanted everything, and I also wanted to do everything right.

There was one problem, however, where could I to go to get this baptism?

I could not ask the Catholic priest who came to administer a quick mass every Sunday in the small chapel of the prison. His catechism denied full immersion. I could not go to the prison commander and ask him to organise a special full immersion baptism for me. I would probably get locked up in solitary for my troubles. Trapped as I was, I decided that I would have to improvise.

As soon as the cell door opened, I made my way to the showers. There I stood under the water cascading down onto me from the showerhead and baptised myself in the name of the Father, The Son and The Holy Spirit.

Maybe some would call this sacrilegious, and maybe some would call it plain stupid, but God did not seem to mind, in fact quite the reverse. There and then I was filled with the Holy Spirit, and for a while I was left burbling like a madman curled up on the floor of the shower as unspeakable joy filled me.

I could not contain myself. Every time I opened my mouth I wanted to talk about the love of God. Words could not contain my joy, I was overflowing with ecstasy. I found myself some paper and wrote page after page of joy-filled gibberish. Everyone I spoke to I needed to convince that Jesus was God and that there was unspeakable joy for all those who chose to follow Him.

Naturally word quickly got around that one of the Englishmen had got some drugs, and it was not long before I was accosted by a group of prisoners, some of them with knives.

'Where are the drugs and how are you getting them?' I was asked threateningly.

'It's not drugs,' I replied, laughing, too full of life to worry about being carved up by drug-starved fellow prisoners. 'It's the love of God that has filled me.'

I explained to them that I had repented of my sins and asked the Holy Spirit to come into my life, and now I was free and saved. Incredulity appeared on all their faces.

'It's true,' I said, 'search me if you want.'

I was subject to a quick search, and all the time I harangued them with the Gospel.

'Jesus loves you,' I kept telling them, over and over again, until finally they decided that I had gone completely crazy, and left me alone.

Unable to get through to anyone I climbed onto my bunk and covered myself with my blanket. There I shivered in delight under the onslaught of love that God had unleashed upon me, and after a while I thought that I was going to die from the sheer joy of it.

'Lord,' I cried, 'you will have to stop because I will die if you continue.'

The Spirit drew away from me slightly, and in the pain of Him leaving I cried out in desperation.

'No, please, do not leave me!'

The Spirit came back, and once again I felt as though I would die from being loved too much.

It was during this time that I also had a recurring vision, the content of which I have never mentioned to anyone else from that day to this, not even my wife. It is the only thing I have ever kept from her, the one thing in my life that is completely between me and God. I have not mentioned it to anyone else because the content of what I saw is all together too incredible and impossible to imagine ever coming true. I have never even alluded to it until now. To even speak about it to anyone would make me feel as if I was uttering something conceited and at the same time betraying a trust. Joseph got himself in deep trouble by uttering out loud something that should perhaps, with the benefit of hindsight, have been kept to himself. I have to be honest and also say that if I did disclose the contents of my vision, and they failed to come true, I would feel like a fool.

Yet... I am a proponent of the wisdom that states that if God asks you to do something, or get involved in something that seems too incredible or far-fetched for you to ever imagine happening, you wait until He keeps telling you, in a way that you know will never go away, and then you do it, hoping and praying all the while that you have got it right. This is what I will do. I will write a letter and post it to myself; I will then only open it in the presence of witnesses after the event has occurred. This way, I will keep face if I am wrong, and God will get the glory if what I saw in prison proves to be correct.

My Bible also succoured me during this time, and one passage in particular managed to reflect what was going on inside me.

1 John: Chapter 4: 7-21

Dear friends, let us love one another, for love comes from God. Everyone who loves has been born of God and knows God.

Whoever does not love does not know God, because God is love.

This is how God showed his love among us: He sent his one and only Son into the world that we might live through him.

This is love: not that we loved God, but that he loved us and sent his Son as an atoning sacrifice for our sins.

Dear friends, since God so loved us, we also ought to love one another. No one has ever seen God; but if we love one another, God lives in us and his love is made complete in us.

We know that we live in him and He in us, because he has given us of his Spirit. And we have seen and testify that the Father has sent his Son to be the Saviour of the world.

If anyone acknowledges that Jesus is the Son of God, God lives in him and he in God.

And so we know and rely on the love God has for us. God is love. Whoever lives in love lives in God, and God in Him.

In this way, love is made complete among us so that we will have confidence on the day of judgement, because in this world we are like him.

There is no fear in love. But perfect love drives out fear, because fear has to do with punishment. The one who fears is not made perfect in love.

We love because he first loved us.

If anyone says, "I love God", yet hates his brother, he is a liar. For anyone who does not love his brother, whom he has seen, cannot love God, whom he has not seen.

And he has given us this command: Whoever loves God must also love his brother.

The love of God that John was trying to impart to the reader I empathised with, and although the true depth and complexity of his words are going to take me a lifetime to comprehend in their entirety, maybe never, I decided that the spirit behind them was the same one that I had been given. I had been given the honour of having God Himself come to abide in my heart, and although I have never really conducted myself as though this was true, it was true nevertheless.

Only one thing disappointed me during these early days of my salvation. I found that I was completely unable to convince anyone around me that what had happened to me was real, that a miracle of grace truly had been wrought in my soul. This is something I have had to come to terms with in my walk with God ever since.

It seemed to me to be such a terrible shame that something as powerful and glorious as what had happened inside me was completely invisible to everyone else. I wanted to take out the event and lay it before my fellow prisoners' eyes, to show them the before and after photograph of my soul, but of course that was impossible. Since then I have sadly accepted that no amount of conviction or determined argument on my part has ever been able to convince anyone who did not want to listen.

I was to learn that this is the subtle humour of salvation to those who experience it. Only those to whom God gives ears to hear, understand what it is that is being said to them. To everyone else it is gibberish, as if the person talking is on drugs. Maybe you, dear reader, are tempted to believe? Maybe something in you is warming to the idea that God might care about you? Love you even? I can give you no proof. Only the proof of a life saved, a life pulled from disaster into something all together different. That is all I have, all I can give. If you choose to believe or not, that is completely up to you, yet I pray that you do. I pray that everyone reading this book will be touched in a way that will give Glory to Him. I can offer you and Him nothing else.

*

It was gradually accepted in the prison population that I was now a religious freak, and someone only to be talked to if you wanted to discuss the fate of your eternal soul. How I wish I could say that since the moment God came into my life I had walked a good clean walk, but I cannot. I improved considerably, and I would like to think that every year since my salvation I have become more like the man He wants me to be. It has been a long and bloody process. A road travelled that has left behind me many tears and sorrows, as well as a huge amount of joy and satisfaction.

Back then I had no concept of exactly what it was that I had been called to, or the fact that there were to be sacrifices made in order to keep me in the grace of God. All I knew was that I was now different, that God Himself had spoken to me and chosen me for something special. Exactly what to do, or how to behave, I was clueless; all I had was a conscience that was still trying to come to terms with being reactivated, and my own garbled mind to decipher the way forward.

I do not wish to make any excuses as to my conduct after receiving the Spirit, and neither do I believe that I was mentally certifiable, but I do think that it would be fair to say that I was not in a good psychological or mental state. I was still emotionally very vulnerable, and prone to bouts of depression and chronic self-doubt. My experiences before and during the Legión had left their mark upon me, and it was going to take many years before I could convincingly decide that I had reached a place where I could comfortably call myself "normal". Something those who know me might yet beg to differ with!

Yet the change was undeniable. I was different, and anytime since I have ever doubted God or His love for me, the first place I have gone for support and help is the memory of my experience in the Castillo. The remembrance of it is as alive in me now as it was then, and I have never been able to doubt the fact that what happened in those few days was of eternal consequence for me.

Life continued in spite of what had happened to me.

Paul got himself into deep water with the prisoners he was mixing with, and came to me asking if we could be put back in the same cell together. I agreed, and it was good to be friends again.

Not everything finished as well. While in prison there were at least two suicide attempts. One friend in the cell down from me drank a litre of bleach and died a few days later in hospital. Another tied his own hands behind his back using a belt and threw himself head first off the top bunk in the middle of the night. He fractured his skull and, after hospital, was sent to a lunatic asylum.

Our own sentencing seemed to be taking forever, but eventually we were told that we were going before a military court soon. The day arrived and we were handcuffed and driven to a local barracks where we sat before a general and two other very senior officers. I was sentenced to six months and ordered to be court-martialled from the Legión. I was disappointed that I was not going to be given the opportunity to clear my name back at the Tercio, but pleased that at last I knew my sentence.

Upon getting back to the prison we were immediately transferred to the condemned section, and I found myself back sharing a cell with only Paul and José for company. José had not changed, even though he, like Paul, had had his fingers burnt in his attempt to set himself up as a dealer. There were men who were prepared to inflict serious injury in order to protect their racket, and both Paul and José had barely escaped severe injury.

There was very little to do apart from eat, sleep, read and smoke. I also found time to add to my tattoos. One prisoner was a skilled artist, and made himself a tattooing machine by using a motor from a tape recorder, some wire, the plastic outer casing of a ball point pen and a needle. He wired it into the light bulb hanging from the roof of his cell and charged us cigarettes for his services. I got a small image of Christ on my stomach and the word "Pelotón" on my left arm. I was strangely proud of the fact that I had completed five months of Pelotón and was still alive.

I also managed to rescue a battered young kitten that had found its way into the prison. It was barely alive and so thin you could see each one of its ribs. It had scars all over its face and body from being beaten, and I wondered whether it would live out the week when I first saw it. I fed it scraps of meat from my own plate and bought it milk, and gradually it filled out and got better. It left as soon as it came, coming back to visit me once or twice before disappearing for good.

Strangely it was good to be back together again with Paul and José. By now there was a familiarity in our relationship, and although José was still as cunning and manipulative as ever I had got used to him. He was continually trying to convince himself and us that because we had all received the same sentence we would be sent on our way when we were let out of the prison gates. Once again I was unsure as to whether his optimism was well placed, but even I wondered what they would do with us. We had been sentenced to six months, and by now we had completed more than that including our time in Pelotón.

The Legión would not want us back, surely? Not after what we had done.

*

Called to the commandant's office one day we were told that we were to be released back into the care of the local Legión barracks in Las Palmas to await our expulsion papers. Before we knew what was happening we were travelling back down the hill in a Land Rover towards Las Palmas, fully expecting there to be someone there with a bundle of papers to sign and an aeroplane ticket home.

When we got to the barracks we were again disappointed. It was an old rundown barracks manned by a small group of disinterested legionarios. The captain in charge was not expecting us, and told us that we would have to wait until he heard from Fuerteventura as to what to do with us. It was only a week until Christmas, so we did what we had become used to doing; we waited for the wheels of the Spanish Army's justice system to slowly wind itself around another turn.

One day we discovered to our joy that we were allowed passes in and out of the barracks, and we quickly made use of them. We made our way to the Playa Del Ingles and had a few beers, marvelling at our new found freedom.

On Christmas Day I persuaded Paul and José to come with me to the local church. There were only us and two or three others there in what was a very rundown area. I found the emotion of it all too much, and much to the surprise of the priest, broke down in tears. I cried like I had never cried before. Deep sobs clawed their way from the bottom of my soul, and afterwards I felt lighter. It was not going to be the last time that my weary and ravaged soul was to find healing this way. Paul and José got up and walked out halfway through, but I stayed to the end, emptying my pockets into the collection plate when it passed.

*

Only a couple of days before New Year we were informed that we were to be sent back to Fuerteventura. We were completely astonished at this news. We had not expected this at all.

'What is to happen to us when we get back there?' we asked the captain.

He had no idea. Our worst fear was that we would be sent back to Pelotón, but the captain assured us that that was impossible.

'You have been sentenced,' he said with a smile, 'they cannot imprison you again. The most likely thing to happen will be that you will be sent back to your company to await the final court martial papers, then you will be flown home.'

Paul was infuriated by the news. He wanted to go home, and obtained a pass for himself the following day. He said that he was only going out to make a phone call, but I knew that he would not come back, and he didn't. I found out later that he had applied for a temporary passport from the British Consul by claiming to be a holidaymaker who had lost his, and flew home with money wired to him by his family.

The captain asked me where he had gone and I shrugged my shoulders.

I could tell that he was curious as to why I had remained behind, and maybe he had been expecting me to desert again, but I had decided that this chance to go back to my company might be the opportunity I needed to clear my name. Surprisingly José also decided to stay.

'I have nowhere else to go,' he explained. 'If I fail to go back I will be hiding from them for the rest of my life, this way I will get my expulsion papers and won't have to look over my shoulder for the rest of my life.'

When the time came to board the ferry back to Fuerteventura, I cannot deny that my heart was in my mouth, and several times I wondered whether I had made the right decision. The only assumption I could come to as to the real reason I was going back, other than as a way of trying to atone for my past mistakes, was because I felt like it was the right thing to do. For most of the journey there I prayed that my gut instinct was right, and I was not opening up a whole new Pandora's box of trouble for myself.

We were greeted at the docks by a military policeman, who after inspecting our papers quickly marched us up the road to the main entrance. It was disconcerting to be back on such familiar ground, and I felt curiously disjointed and out of place. My heart was beating wildly as we were questioned by the officer on guard, who frustratingly declared, after a few phone calls, that no one was expecting us.

Maybe that was why the captain in Las Palmas was surprised that I had not left with Paul? If I had done another runner the Legión would merely strike me from their records and a lot of paperwork would have been binned. As it was, we were marched back up to our old company and the bemused faces of the NCOs and officers on duty.

The captain called to see me. He was new to the company and initially was angry at my reappearance, incredulous as to why I had returned. I assured him that all I wanted was a chance to clear my name and the ability to leave with a vestige of honour.

'Just give me a chance,' I said. 'I will work hard, and I promise that there will be no more trouble. If I had wanted to leave I would have taken my chance with Paul in Gran Canaria.'

Finally he nodded and dismissed me.

'I will be watching you very closely, Mark,' he said as I exited his office. 'Do not let me down.'

I was quickly assigned a bed, and within a few days I was back in the groove of military life. José was packed off to the administrative company where he managed to secure a job as a waiter in the officers' mess. I did not miss him and felt lighter in my soul for not having him around. Especially so after speaking to a military policeman in the bar one night who told me that they would never have found me if it had not been for the tip-off they had received about us being in the port on Tenerife. I could not help smiling when I remembered how José had slunk off for a while when we were hiding in the cave on Montana Rojo and Paul was down in the village trying to get some money in order to phone home.

Had José ratted on us?

I was surprised to discover that I did not really care. What had happened had happened. Besides, if we had not been caught then I would not have ended up at Calvary crucifying the Christ. In a way José had served the purposes of God, and I had no room in my heart for anger when I weighed up what I had discovered because of his treachery. It was probably true to say that I was eternally in his debt, so instead of plotting revenge I concentrated on my soldiering.

At first most of the NCOs were reluctant to accept me and started to give me a hard time. I decided that the best thing was to speak to them all individually, explain my predicament, tell them how I had been lied to, and apologise for bringing the company and myself into disrepute. I told them that I wanted this one chance to clear my name. I would soldier as hard as I could, and hopefully when the time came to leave it would not be under too dark a cloud of shame.

Most accepted what I said with good grace, and in the true spirit of Legión comradeship were prepared to give me another chance. One or two were not so forgiving. I remember one corporal who refused to even listen to me. He became a bit of a pain with his constant criticisms and efforts to undermine me. One day, after a few weeks of failing to gain this particular corporal's respect, I heard a sergeant speaking to him.

'You need to back off,' he said, 'he has done his time. All he wants is a chance to leave with a little respect. So far I see no reason not to give him that chance. He is working bloody hard, harder than most.'

The corporal duly left me alone.

Olivedo then reappeared. Apparently he had been away on some course or other. I wondered what mischief he might have in store for me. He called me over to see him and looked me up and down a few times, a quizzical look in his eyes.

'Is it true?' he asked, his face watching mine to see if he could detect any insincerity.

'Is what true, sir?'

'That you have come back purely to clear your name?'

'Yes, sir,' I replied.

'Then we shall see how you conduct yourself, and I will give you a chance.'

Mostly he kept his word and merely watched me. I knew that he was waiting for me to step out of line so he could revert to form, but without Paul and José's influence to distract me, and by my tactics of keeping my head down and doing everything asked of me quickly and without grumbling, I slowly started to win him around.

It was true that sometimes I would get the short straw if a dirty job was to be done, but I reasoned that this was my just desserts and got on with it. Often I would find guard duty sprung on me with only a couple of hours notice because they were shorthanded. Ordinarily it took four or five hours to prepare your kit for guard, but I had taken to preparing mine in readiness anyway, and never seemed to be caught out. I put every fortuitous happening like this down to God's providence.

Most of my fellow legionarios accepted me without many qualms, and I was quite surprised to discover that I was respected and slightly feared by most of them. I asked a friend of mine, a fellow foreigner from Portugal, what the score was.

'Are you kidding?' he said. 'You survived five months in Pelotón and three months in the Castillo, that alone means that you deserve a certain amount of respect, then they find out that when you had the opportunity to go home you came back here to clear your name! Within a few days you have all the NCOs singing your praises instead of beating you black and blue, and you're always off in some corner alone to read your Bible.'

'Why would any of that worry them?' I asked, realising that I did find everything far easier than before, but prepared to Pelotón, normal Legión life was like a picnic.

'Because it means that no one understands you!' he said with a laugh. 'Most have decided that you're crazy, and a man to be avoided unless there is going to be fight when they would rather you were on their side.'

I shuddered. Not quite the reputation I was looking for, but it did mean that I was left alone most of the time. Time I used to think about the future, and to get on with reading my Bible.

I prayed often, asking God to help me make it through the next few weeks or months, or however long it took to sort my expulsion papers out, but I found that one thing began to trouble me more than most as my time as a soldier dragged on.

What happens if we were to be sent to war and I was ordered to kill? Should I obey my orders and fight? I was now a Christian, and the Bible quite clearly stated that to kill is a sin and I should love my enemy.

I searched the Bible for an answer and found it.

In Luke, chapter 3, verses 14–15, some soldiers come to see John the Baptist and asked him how they were to conduct themselves. His answer to them provided me with mine.

'Don't extort money,' John replied, 'don't accuse people falsely, and be content with your pay.'

What struck me was that he did not tell them to leave the army because it was an immoral occupation. He merely stated that they were to behave with decency. Likewise in Luke, chapter 7, verses 1–10, and Matthew, chapter 8, verses 5–13, Jesus is asked by a Roman soldier to heal his servant. Jesus does not condemn the man for being a soldier, even though he is from the occupying force, instead he expresses delight at the faith the soldier has in Him and dutifully heals the sick servant without even stepping into the soldier's house.

In these scriptures I discovered my answer. It did not matter that I was a soldier, what mattered was how I conducted myself as one, so for the most part I worked hard, I was content with my pay and I tried to behave as honourably as I could. I also discovered later that the literal translation of "Thou Shalt Not Kill" is "Thou Shalt Not Murder", a subtle difference, especially if you are a soldier.

I wish I could tell you that I did not smoke any more drugs, or get involved in a few things I should not have done, but I cannot. I have to be honest, and maybe the only excuse I can give is that in the circumstances I was in then, with no one to look to for moral guidance and spiritual instruction other than my own fragile conscience, and not fully knowing what had happened to me other than something out of the ordinary, I was often tempted to stray from the path of righteousness. Even the language I use in this book to describe my spiritual experiences was unknown to me then. Mostly I was making it all up as I went along.

I make no excuse. I should have been stronger, and gradually as the days and weeks went by, I did improve. I gained in faith, and my love for my Saviour grew as I read and reread the Gospels. My conscience started convincing me that there was no more food for my soul on the tables from which I had previously eaten. Instead I realised that I was now able to feast at the banquet of grace laid out by the Lord, and nothing has ever had quite the same flavour, or ever felt as wholly satisfying since.

A few more weeks flew by, and the company brigada called to see me. He was a handsome man with a reputation as a soldier's soldier. Slim, with a fierce smile and intense eyes, and like the Brigada of Pelotón he had many small and crude homemade tattoos on his arms. It was obvious that here was another man from a shady background of whom the Legión had managed to make something. He told me that in two or three weeks' time the papers were going to arrive and I was to be flown home. He organised my back pay and talked me through the paperwork.

'Where do you live?' he asked.

I shrugged my shoulders, hoping to mask the sudden panic that had risen in my heart, as various questions came rushing at me in the face of this not unexpected news. Where was home? Would I be welcome back in Yorkshire? Did I even want to go? I had spent so much of my energy working at soldiering, reading my Bible and not on planning for my future, that I was now surprised at the suddenness of something arriving I should have expected.

The brigada must have seen my confusion.

'I tell you what,' he said with a smile, 'I will get you a ticket to the "Paseo De Gracia" in Barcelona. That is not far from the border with France. From there you might find a quick journey back home.'

'The "Walk of Grace",' I replied, smiling at the holy irony of the name. 'Yes, that will do very well, thank you.'

*

Before I was to finally get my hands on my plane ticket the Legión was to throw me one last swerve ball.

A couple of days after my meeting with the brigada I was called in to see the lieutenant colonel of our regiment. I had only ever seen him from afar before, but up as close to him as I was when he called me into his office, he struck me as a man cut from the same cloth as almost all the senior officers in the Legión. He was tall and aristocratic with an undisguised air of menace about him, as if warning you that he had the power of life and death held in his hands. He was not a man to trifle with, none of them were.

I was expecting a final reprimand before being handed my expulsion papers, but as he continued speaking it suddenly dawned on me that he was offering me a job. Not just any job, he was offering me a chance to become a "Gastador". These were the showmen of the Legión, specialising in spectacular and flamboyant gun drill for military parades. It was a good posting, and came with perks and the opportunity to travel. Apparently he had noticed me at a recent regimental parade. I was surprised that no one had told him that I was a deserter awaiting expulsion.

'I'm sorry, sir,' I replied, 'but I am awaiting my expulsion papers.'

He brushed this comment away with a flick of his pen.

'Would you like the job?' he asked.

I was completely flabbergasted now. I had no answer to give.

'Go away and think about it,' he said.

I went back to my company hut. There the Company Brigada was waiting to see me. I told him about the conversation.

'You have gained quite a reputation since you got back from the Castillo,' he said, smiling.

'How can I stay?' I asked. 'I have been court-martialled.'

'You wouldn't,' he replied, 'but someone else, looking just like you will be entered onto the Legión payroll.'

The penny dropped. They would sign me on under a different name, and although Mark Gee would have ostensibly gone home, another foreigner would have signed on in his place.

'The question you have to ask yourself,' the brigada stated, 'is whether you want to make this your career.' His eyes then grew sad and melancholic. 'I feel like I have been here a thousand years, and that is a hell of a long time, do you understand what I am trying to say?'

I looked into his eyes and nodded as I remembered the Moroccan who signed back on again only two weeks after leaving. He had wanted to go and establish a farm in the foothills of the Atlas Mountains to breed goats, but he could no longer cope with the outside world. The Legión had institutionalised him. I knew instinctively that if I signed on again that would be it. I would never leave. Maybe that would have been an option before I came to know the Lord, but now? Is that really what God wanted from me?

'The Paseo De Gracia sounds like the best option,' I said, and the brigada nodded his approval.

*

The day of my expulsion came through. I had to hand in my uniform the day before, so I went out into Puerto Del Rosario and bought myself some civilian clothes. The shoes felt too light on my feet after nothing but boots, and the clothes seemed too flimsy. I hoped my future life would not be so insubstantial.

The morning of my expulsion I was in my civilian clothes and ordered to one side of the company as they fell in. After roll call I shook hands with almost all the company, including the corporals and sergeants; it seemed that everyone wanted to wish me well. I picked up my holdall and made my way towards the front gate. I had an aeroplane ticket and just short of three hundred pounds in my pocket.

Walking past the line for breakfast, someone shouted out.

'Where are you going now, Mark?'

I did not see who it was, and I could not recognise the voice, but without thinking I shouted back:

'I am going to the land of milk and honey.'

The Promised Land?

That seemed like as good a destination as anyone has ever set themselves.

EPILOGUE

Walking With the Christ

Outside the main gate I turned around and had one final look at the place that had held so much pain and joy for me. The Spanish Flag fluttered lazily in the breeze against the backdrop of the large whitewashed barracks frontage. The guard on duty eyed me suspiciously; probably unsure as to whom I was in my civilian clothes. I was suddenly filled with great emotion. I wanted to let him know that being a legionario had been one of the most significant periods of my life. I wanted to tell the whole barracks that if it had not been for them, used as a tool by the mighty hand of God to break what was a proud and stubborn soul, I would not now know the Lord Jesus Christ as my personal Saviour. That would have probably got me a belt around the head by the duty officer. The Legión was not big on emotion, so instead I sent out a short prayer of thanks.

I thanked God for making himself known to me in that most miraculous of ways, and I also thanked Him for giving me the adventure my heart had longed for all my life. I had had no idea what would happen to me when I had signed on the dotted line in Ronda, and even I, with my huge thirst for adventure and head filled with hopeless romance, would never have been able to dream up such a story as I had just been in. It was everything I had ever wanted and more.

However, I also felt sad.

How I wished I had been standing there with a good conduct letter in my pocket having completed my contract honourably, but that was not meant to be. I had let the Legión down, and I will never be able to alter that. There will forever be a black mark against my name in the Legión list. Maybe I had gone some way to clearing my reputation in the last few months, I hoped so, but the world is not as forgiving as God, and now I could expect nothing better than my own personal sense of fulfilment at having tried to serve the last few months of my time respectably.

I also had to ask myself one thing in that moment as the threat of nostalgia threatened to swamp me. Would I go through it all again to know what I know now? Would I suffer the shame and the pain in order to hear once again the voice of Jesus Christ as He forgave me from the cross?

I laughed at the futility of the question.

Of course I would. It was worth every bruise, every kick in the teeth and every tear shed. I honestly thought that I had got away considerably lightly considering what God had to organise in order to get me to my knees. It was, and still is now, an awesome memory to have available to me, and it has sustained me through many dark moments of doubt.

The awe-inspiring way He fashioned my salvation was similar to the way a sculptor will look at a block of marble and see trapped within it the figure of the man he wants to bring to life. He will then set to work with his hammer and chisel in order to release his creation into the light. This is what God did for me. He saw something in me worth working on; and slowly but surely He brought me to life. So meticulous and dedicated was His planning, and so determined and ruthless was God's desire to see me saved, that the thought of it sometimes leaves me breathless. God - for no other reason other than He decided to do it - opened up for me the gates of salvation and led me in.

May God forgive me if I ever forget that it was He, and only He, who made me His man. I can hold no credit in my heart in the light of His glorious mercy. I have nothing of which to boast, but in God's grace. I was a wretched man, lost in a morass of sin and shame, searching for a reason to exist in the midst of a world I had come to distrust and hate with a passion.

Now look at me!

Now I was on my way to the "Land of Milk and Honey", and only God Himself knew what sort of adventure that was going to be.

*

I made it to the Paseo De Gracia without incident. I wanted to see it, I was curious as to what a street looked like that called itself by such an auspicious name. There, to my amazement, I found a bus at the kerbside ready to leave for London. I asked the driver if I could buy a ticket and he said yes. I arrived back in Yorkshire three days and no sleep later.

*

My fingers have hovered over the keyboard at this point for a good few weeks, wondering whether or not to continue with my story, because continue it does, and I have to admit that some parts of it have been no less interesting than the adventure you have only just read about. Unfortunately I have decided that this book ends here. Not because my walk with God ended, far from it. I am still walking with the Christ, still in love with the God who rescued me all those years ago, and still gloriously perplexed as to why He should have bothered with me. The reason I cannot tell you about it yet, is simply because I have not yet reached the end of the next book. Maybe I never will!

What I will tell you is that I found reconciliation with my mother and Colin, who thanks to God had also become committed Christians while I was in Spain, a true miracle of grace. They prayed for me as I sat with them in the living room, and I felt a glorious filling of the Spirit as they did so, as if God was washing away the tiredness and dust of my long journey home. They also graciously allowed me to stay with them until I could figure out what it was God wanted of me; a lovely and generous thing to do.

During my time with my parents, I fell in love again with Yorkshire and the surrounding moors and woods of my home village, Meltham. Nothing gave me more joy in the following weeks than running or walking in the stunning countryside. Once I managed the arduous run up to the top of Wessenden Head, and perched as I was on the top of West Yorkshire, whipped at by the wild wind that perennially inhabits the heather-strewn harshness surrounding the bold granite outcrop, I lifted up my hands and sang out my praises to God, wondering as I did so what was going to become of me in the months and years ahead.

This time I did not hear the audible voice of God in response to my praises, but I did hear Him whispering into my soul with that calm assuring voice only He has.

'Everything is going to be all right, Mark,' He said, 'everything is going to be just fine.'

And it has been. I am now married to a beautiful woman who has born me two gorgeous children, a girl and a boy, and when I am praying early in the morning, while everyone else in the house is still fast asleep, I thank Him for them. I also thank God for the Legión and everything that has befallen me since, because the truth is, I am who I am because of what happened to me there. As painful as it was, it has brought me to where I am now, and I would not change my life with anyone else on the planet. I am a happy man, a blessed man, a true product of the mighty Grace of God.

Regarding my ongoing walk with God, I attend a Baptist Church in the City of Coventry where I have made my home. It is a lovely church full of great people, and I am deeply attached to it. Amazingly, and to their great credit, they have accepted me into their midst – tattoos and all - and they even let me stand up and have my say every now and then - amazing!

I would dearly love to tell you that on my search for the Promised Land I went on to become a mighty man of God, leading many souls to salvation all over the world, but I cannot. I am just a normal guy trying to make his way in the world while honouring his God. This book is nothing more than me wanting to give something back, to let the world know that there is a God and that He is still able to perform miracles. It's a bit late in the writing, but here it is nevertheless, I hope you have enjoyed it.

*

Your response:

Maybe you will be like my fellow prisoners in the Castillo San Francisco Del Risco and choose not to listen to me, choose not to believe the glorious good news I recount to you here? That is your choice; God is not in the habit of forcing Himself on anyone who does not want to know the truth.

Now that you have read the book, the question you do have to ask yourself is what excuse you will make to avoid God when you put the book down and get on with your life, because now you will not be able to plead ignorance before the throne of God on the Day of Judgement. I have told you the truth, I have shown you a way to a door, and now all you have to do is make your way to it and knock.

Go on! What have you got to lose?

If – as I hope and pray you do - you choose to knock on the door of Heaven, I can promise you this. You will not be disappointed, glorious wonders are contained therein, and what is more, you will have made this writer a very happy man indeed.

May God bless you in whatever you choose!

23671432R00102

Printed in Great Britain
by Amazon